CHOCOLATE...
IS MY KRYPTONITE

FEEDING YOUR FEELINGS
HOW TO SURVIVE THE FORCES OF FOOD

CHOCOLATE...
IS MY KRYPTONITE

FEEDING YOUR FEELINGS
HOW TO SURVIVE THE FORCES OF FOOD

MATTHEW S. KEENE, MD

SAGUARO PUBLISHING

Litchfield Park, Arizona

CHOCOLATE IS MY KRYPTONITE
FEEDING YOUR FEELINGS/HOW TO SURVIVE THE FORCES OF FOOD

Published by:
Saguaro Publishing
P.O. Box 457
Litchfield Park, AZ 85340

Cover design and printing by Tri Star Printing and Visual Communications, Phoenix, AZ

Keene, Matt
    Chocolate is my kryptonite...feeding your feelings / how to survive the forces of food

Includes index

ISBN: 0-9659847-2-9
LCCN: 97-69389

To Anita

The wife who loves me
The friend who supports me
The woman who inspires me

About The Author

Matthew S. Keene, MD is the founder & director of Feeding Your Feelings: a multi-disciplinary team of health care professionals dedicated to the management of compulsive overeating through the development of human potential. He graduated with honors from Georgetown University School of Medicine and received his psychiatric residency training at the Cleveland Clinic Foundation. A national consultant, trainer, and psychopharmacologist, Dr. Keene currently practices psychiatry in Phoenix, AZ.

Acknowledgments

I wish to express my deepest thanks and appreciation to Robin Piper. Her wisdom led me out of the Stone Age, convincing me that compulsive overeating is much more than just a simple matter of willpower. Her guidance gave this work life and substance. Her strength and testimony has touched the hearts of thousands. Many, many thanks.

Thanks also to Drs. Kaveh Khajavi, Eric Heidenreich, and David Stone for their perpetual encouragement; and to Drs. John Sorboro, Elizabeth Dolgas, and Toni Carmen for giving me the opportunity of a lifetime. Also, special thanks to Donna Sterrett for her skillful proofreading.

Lastly, and above all, I would like to express my gratitude to my parents, Joyce and Kenneth Keene. Their support has been undying and their devotion unparalleled. I love them more than words can say.

Contents

Preface

I have a confession to make. Like the majority of my colleagues, I once believed that weight control was simply a matter of willpower. I thought, "Eat less. Exercise more. Blah blah blah. It's that simple." Well, I was wrong!

My belief changed in September of 1992 when I began working with a dynamic social worker named Robin. The hospital brought her on board to organize a new eating disorder treatment program. Her expertise came from the heart; because not only was Robin an eating disorder specialist, she was also a recovering food addict. Yes, a food addict.

At first, the very notion of food addiction seemed ridiculous to me. I wondered, "How could such a vibrant young woman like Robin ever have a problem with food? How could she possibly become addicted to processed carbohydrates, sugar, and excess fat?" In short, I was a skeptic.

However, I soon learned that Robin was not alone. Dozens of fellow compulsive overeaters shared her concept of physical addiction to binge food. But unlike Robin, they weren't in recovery. Their lives continued to be controlled by food, and they desperately wanted help—my help! Not because I championed their cause. Heck, I didn't even understand it. But simply because they trusted Robin, and she trusted me to provide them with sound medical treatment.

Soon thirty compulsive overeaters were under my care. In order to help them, I began reading every text, journal, and article I could find on the subject. What I discovered astonished me.

In brief, compulsive overeaters suffer from a deficiency in serotonin: the body's calming chemical. When serotonin levels are low, people feel sad, tense, or irritable. Surprisingly, binge food provides a way to temporarily increase the body's supply of serotonin. Thus, without even realizing it, compulsive overeaters binge in order to literally feed their feelings and "medicate" their sickly serotonin systems. It's the only way their bodies know how to emotionally survive.

Unfortunately, persistent overeating is mired with complications including obesity, bulimia, and major depression. In fact, over the long run, compulsive overeating serves to decrease serotonin even further.

Relax, you aren't expected to understand, or for that matter, to have even heard of serotonin. It will all be explained in the chapters that follow. For now, the most important thing to realize is that compulsive overeating is a disease that can be treated!

Through a combination of feelings management, a revolutionary food plan, and occasionally medication, compulsive overeating can be stopped in it's tracks. I've seen it happen hundreds of times. Lives are completely restored as recovery rejuvenates the soul. It's nothing short of a miracle, and I thank my clients for allowing me to share in their experiences.

Chocolate is My Kryptonite provides the latest information on managing both the biology and psychology of compulsive overeating. Best of all, it does so without a lot of technical mumbo jumbo. This book is for the 18 million compulsive overeaters who want a guide to recovery that is complete yet fun to read. It is for the family, friends, and physicians of those who suffer from this deadly disease; because understanding the problem is the key to finding its solution. This book is really for anyone who struggles with the most prevalent drug known to man—FOOD!

Chapter 1

Are You a Compulsive Overeater?

"Give me a dozen donuts when I'm craving, and I'll show that Cocoa Puff Bird what coo-coo really is."

- Laura

"If I lost one pound for every diet I've tried, I'd be lighter than air. Too bad I'm still thirty pounds overweight."

- Sandi

"I hate the way I eat. I hate the way I look. Mostly, I hate myself."

- Dan

"I have six kids and weigh over two hundred pounds. My friends call me Supermom. **Chocolate is my Kryptonite.**"

- Ellen

Can you identify with these comments shared by my clients? Maybe like them, you've heard all the rhetoric and tried all the remedies, yet you continue to feel powerless over food. Loved ones tell you that you are "weak and lack willpower." Strangers and so-called friends quietly remark that you are "lazy and have no self-respect." Your doctor chastises you and asks, "Do you have a death wish?"

Deep in your heart and soul you know you are not at fault. But with every diet, cream, or pill you try, the cycle of bingeing and weight gain continues. It seems as though you just can't win, so you begin to fear the worst: "Maybe I am shameful, worthless, and hopeless. Why even bother trying to control my appetite? Why not take solace with my one true friend–food? Why not take another bite?"

STOP! LOOK! LISTEN! But above all read on. After years of feeling driven, compelled, and mesmerized by food, there is now proof that compulsive overeating is not a character flaw. It's a distinct medical illness!

To Eat Or Not To Eat? That Is The Question

What is compulsive overeating? Ask one hundred people and you will probably get one hundred different answers. But for the purposes of this book, compulsive overeating is defined as: *the rapid, persistent, and uncontrollable consumption of highly processed carbohydrates (HPCs), sugar, and excess fat that leads to worsening physical and emotional consequences.*

I'm sure you already know some of the physical consequences of compulsive overeating. They include diabetes, hypertension, heart disease, arthritis, and the health related dangers of unsound diets and purging.

The emotional consequences, however, are much broader and less recognized. They include poor self-esteem, decreased assertiveness, family fighting, depression, and the use of food as a guardian against unwanted thoughts or feelings.

But the main consequence of compulsive overeating is WEIGHT–too much of it, that is. Okay, so maybe it's not that plain and simple; not all compulsive overeaters are overweight. Maybe you have the metabolism of a gazelle–you graze constantly, never gaining an ounce–yet your thoughts and feelings are ruled by food. Or maybe you thwart weight gain through dangerous methods of purging. But if you are like most compulsive overeaters, by the time you realize and accept your problem with food, the result is all too obvious–the scale is your enemy!

Don't get me wrong. Not every overweight person is a compulsive overeater. In fact, only 20-40 percent of overweight individuals are considered binge eaters. Still, this represents approximately 18 million people in the United States alone. Are you one of them? The questionnaire that follows will help you answer this question.

Place an **X** beside the appropriate statement if you feel it applies. There are no right or wrong answers, so please put down your initial reaction.

Part I

1. ____ I am 20% or more over my ideal body weight (refer to Appendix).

2. ____ I eat large amounts of food in a short period of time (at least twice per week).

3. ____ I have difficulty eating just 1 or 2 bites of something sweet and frequently eat more than planned.

4. ____ I eat when I don't feel hungry.

5. ____ I continue to eat after I feel full.

6. ____ I feel hungry all of the time.

7. ____ I think about food most of the time.

8. ____ I get irresistible cravings to eat certain foods.

9. ____ I hide my favorite foods to prevent others from eating them.

10. ____ I am disgusted with the way I eat.

Part II

1. _____ I feel guilty eating certain foods.

2. _____ I prefer an average meal and great dessert over a great meal with no dessert.

3. _____ Cookies, cakes, and candy make me feel better.

4. _____ I often fill up on bread at restaurants.

5. _____ I eat less fruits and vegetables at mealtime to save room for bread or dessert.

6. _____ I sleep better if I eat a snack before bed.

7. _____ I awaken in the middle of the night with thoughts of food.

8. _____ I have problems with my social, emotional, or physical health because of binge food.

Part III

Which of the following have you tried in an effort to lose weight or curb your appetite?

_____ medically unsubstantiated diets (i.e., grapefruit, crash, rice, etc.)

_____ fasting

_____ excess exercise

_____ water pills (diuretics)

_____ laxatives

_____ vomiting

Part IV

I eat when I am . . .

_____ nervous	_____ jealous
_____ preoccupied	_____ angry
_____ feeling sorry for myself	_____ rejected
_____ lonely	_____ shy
_____ tired	_____ guilty
_____ sad	_____ ashamed

How did you do? For most, this questionnaire is self-diagnostic. Part I is a screening set of questions designed to separate those who repeatedly overeat from those who do not. Part II highlights the attitudes and behaviors that are characteristic of those who crave highly processed carbohydrates (HPCs), sugar, and excess fat. If you identified with items in both parts I and II, then it's quite likely you are a compulsive overeater. The more items checked, the greater the likelihood. Part III is a checklist of the dangerous reduction methods used when the cycle of overeating and weight gain has spiraled to desperate levels. The physical consequences related to these activities are devastating and potentially life threatening. If you are currently engaged in any one of these practices, please seek medical attention before continuing this book. Part IV emphasizes the connection between feeding and feeling. The psychology of compulsive overeating is such that food is often used as an escape from normal, albeit uncomfortable, emotions.

If your responses to these questions alarm you, then perhaps you have taken the first step toward breaking the R.U.T. of compulsive overeating:

> **R**ecognition
> **U**nderstanding
> **T**reatment

Recognizing compulsive overeating as a disease allows you to discard the stereotypes, snake oils, and blinders that prevent successful recovery. Now you can focus on the true face of this deceptive illness. Because **understanding** compulsive overeating provides the inspiration and motivation for the successful **treatment** of this multifaceted disease.

Chapter 2

Food for Thought: The Biology of Compulsive Overeating

Two Strikes and You're Out!

Why do you overeat? That's a simple enough question. Unfortunately, there's just no simple answer. Not long ago, there was considerable confusion regarding the origins of all illnesses. In a time when most maladies were believed caused by spirits, curses, and angry gods, Hypocrites was among the first to propose that disease had a biologic basis. As time passed and society advanced, biologic theories (**nature**) gained popularity, often linking environmental and behavioral factors (**nurture**) to illness. Today such a blend of nature and nurture is responsible for many common ailments, including compulsive overeating. In fact, this coupling of nature and nurture was recently given its own name: the *Two-Hit Hypothesis*. The first hit in this hypothesis is a genetic one; certain hereditary influences make some of us susceptible to specific illnesses, while others are not. The second hit refers to any environmental or behavioral conditions that trigger this genetic susceptibility. Here's how it works.

Although it's not a very appealing thought, we are all just clumps of cells. Each cell contains twenty-six pairs of chromosomes, and every chromosome contains thousands of genes. Genes are responsible for making a specific product that contributes to who we are. Some genes make good durable products, while others make products that are flawed. Imagine two people with two different genes; one makes Levi's and the other makes thin polyester disco-dancing jeans. Both pairs of jeans-genes produce fully functional pants with pockets, zippers, and even some of those fancy-smancy labels. Now let me apologize to the Polyester Growers of America, but let's face facts. The polyester pants are made of an inferior material (the first hit). Next, imagine that these two people are walking along a wooded path and accidentally catch their jeans on a jagged hickory branch. The Levi's absorb the impact, but the polyester jeans tear. The branch influenced the outcome of the product and represents the second hit. Both the first hit (nature/biology) and second hit (nurture/environment) were required to produce this adverse outcome—of course anymore, tearing a hole in your jeans is considered quite stylish.

A more practical analogy is cancer. Many of us are born with genetic predispositions to develop tumors if exposed to certain toxins; however, our friends and neighbors can be exposed to the same poisons and remain healthy. For example, cigarettes are unquestionably the second hit necessary for developing lung cancer; yet we all have an Aunt So&So who has smoked like a chimney for the last eighty years and will probably out live us all.

Smoking is one of many examples in which environment and behavior can impact illness in a negative manner. Fortunately, we are now more aware that environment and behavior can positively alter the course of our health. Exercise and low salt diets can control hypertension, vitamin C can prevent colds, and The Menu For Life can help you recover from compulsive overeating. But I'm getting ahead of myself. Let's get back to the original question, "Why do you overeat?" To answer this, let's first take a closer look at your brain and the "nature" of compulsive overeating.

Neurology 101

Your brain is comprised of millions of living cells called *neurons*. These neurons form a complex weave of tissue that acts as a high-tech communication system. Each neuron is able to transmit an electrical signal, from the top of its little neuron-head to the tip of its little neuron-toes, much like any electrical wire in your home can do. Just as electricity is transformed into video for your TV or sound for your phone, the electrical signals in neurons are also transformed—this time into chemical messengers called *neurotransmitters*. It is these neurotransmitters that facilitate communication between different parts of your brain.

Your brain makes lots of different neurotransmitters. They are stored in something called *vesicles*, which are sort of like tiny cellular houseboats. Let's say one neuron (we'll call it the speaking neuron) needs to speak with its neighbor. To do so, the speaking neuron simply undocks its neurotransmitter-packed vesicles and lets them set sail upon the sea that separates the two. (For those of you who want to impress your friends, this sea is known as the *synaptic cleft*.) Eventually, the neighboring neuron (listening neuron) receives the speaking neuron's neurotransmitters, and alters its actions accordingly.

In some ways, neurons seem to speak to each other by passing messages in a bottle. The neurotransmitters are the message, the vesicle is the bottle, and the synaptic cleft is the sea the message must cross. So if there is something wrong with the neurotransmitters, then the message is garbled and communication between neurons breaks down. Too short a message, and the meaning is vague. Too long a message, and the content is lost.

Neurotransmitter miscommunication plays a role in a number of common diseases. For example, hyperactivity of the neurotransmitter, dopamine, is linked to schizophrenia. Likewise, abnormalities of a different neurotransmitter, acetylcholine, are associated with Alzheimer's disease. But let's not muddy the water with talk of dopamine or acetylcholine. For now, let's focus on the message of the one neurotransmitter that "ain't conversating right" in the brains of compulsive overeaters—*serotonin*.

Serotonin: The Feeding & Feeling Chemical

Serotonin is your body's calming chemical. It promotes a sense of well-being and keeps your mood on an even keel. Experts believe that defects in serotonin produce a spectrum of illnesses. Research supports that the repeated behaviors of the obsessive-compulsive, the suicidal thoughts of the depressed, the panic felt by the anxious, and the alcoholic's urge to drink may all be related to deficiencies in this one powerful neurotransmitter.

Serotonin is stored in several parts of your body, including your gastrointestinal tract, blood cells, and most importantly, your brain. Although serotonin is distributed throughout the entire brain, higher concentrations exist in two crucial areas: the *hypothalamus* and *limbic system*.

The hypothalamus is the "caveman" part of your brain. He makes sure all of your primitive needs are met—"Thog hungry, Thog thirsty, Thog want to meet pretty cave-woman." In other words, the hypothalamus is your *"feeding brain."* It feeds your basic biologic instincts and drives.

The limbic system, on the other hand, is the "Richard Simmons" of your brain—all sensitive and mushy—wanting to give everyone a group hug. The limbic system perceives and expresses your emotions. You can think of it as your *"feeling brain."*

For whatever reason, God decided that these two parts

of the brain should be the best of friends. So he connected them through a vast net of neurons whose primary messenger is serotonin. Unfortunately, a recent study suggests that serotonin levels are more than *four times lower* in compulsive overeaters than in non-binge eaters. So how does this deficiency effect your brain's ability to communicate?

Well, going back to our "message in a bottle" analogy, a disruption of serotonin in the feeding and feeling parts of your brain would make neurotransmitter conversations pretty darn confusing. Confusing enough to mix-up emotion with food? Absolutely. Maybe even confusing enough to cause compulsive overeating? You betcha!

When serotonin is disrupted, your limbic system (the feeling brain) is weakened. You feel depressed and cranky for no good reason. Your hypothalamus (the feeding brain) can sense your discomfort, but being the caveman that he is, can only offer this primitive solution: "eat, EAT, **EAT**!" Yet as primitive and unhealthy as this solution may be, it works! Feeding your feelings temporarily boosts serotonin and makes you feel better. "How?" you ask. Keep reading.

The Tryptophan Express

The body manufactures serotonin from the amino acid, tryptophan. Like all amino acids, tryptophan comes from protein—you know, beef, poultry, fish, even that rubbery tofu stuff. You are probably thinking to yourself, "If I ate a big T-bone with some tofu, I could really make my brain serotonin level soar. Right?" Wrong! Instead, the opposite occurs. Here's why.

In order for tryptophan to reach the brain and be converted into serotonin, it must first hitch a ride on a carrier molecule—all aboard the Brain Train—next stop, the hypothalamus. Protein meals, however, supply your body with several amino acids, not just tryptophan; and all of these amino acids are competing for a ride on the same Brain Train. Unfortunately, tryptophan is the least abundant amino acid. This allows the other amino acids to out number tryptophan and "bully" their way onto the Train. Like a frail elderly woman trying to board a New York subway during rush hour, tryptophan is knocked aside and denied access to the brain. As a result, protein meals cause both your tryptophan and serotonin levels to decline.

So if tryptophan-containing protein can't raise your serotonin level, what can? How about processed carbohydrates which don't contain any tryptophan at all. Make sense? Of course not, but let's just pretend it's another congressional decision.

Research confirms that eating a carbohydrate meal of just two slices of bread with jam will yield a rise in serotonin by a whopping 447 percent; however, a protein-rich chicken breast actually decreases serotonin by 28 percent. Clearly the potential exists to manipulate serotonin levels through diet, especially with carbohydrates, but how?

Officer Insulin

Carbohydrates' ability to influence tryptophan and serotonin levels actually makes perfect medical sense; because even though protein is your source for these chemical wonders, carbohydrates help them reach your brain. Carbohydrates do this by stimulating the release of *insulin* from your pancreas. Insulin acts like a transit cop who disperses the other amino acids out of your bloodstream and clears the way for tryptophan. Without competition, tryptophan has easy access to the Brain Train and hops on board.

It makes sense that if more insulin cops are on the scene, then more tryptophan can climb aboard for conversion into serotonin. In this respect, all carbohydrates are not created equal. Some release the insulin equivalent of Barney Fife, while others release Dirty Harry. And then there are the HPCs and sugar. They can release an entire Swat Team of insulin. Well, I'm running out of police analogies, so let's up the ante and get a bit more technical.

The amount of insulin your pancreas secretes depends on several factors. There are, however, two conditions that greatly increase the release of insulin:

Condition-1: a rapid rise in sugar concentration
Condition-2: consuming several calories at once

Highly processed carbohydrates and sugars are able to fuel both of these conditions, yielding enough insulin cops to fill the set of NYPD Blue–sorry sometimes I can't stop myself. Anyhow, here's how it works.

Condition-1

Commercial processing strips carbohydrates of their complexity, making them far closer to sugar than the whole grain, fruit, or vegetable they once were. When carbohydrates are highly processed, they are just a bite away from becoming sugar. Stick a saltine in your mouth for a few seconds without swallowing, and you'll know exactly what I mean. Suddenly, your salty saltine tastes as sweet as sweet can be. Why? Because your body breaks down HPCs into simple sugar faster than you can say "binge food."

There's just no better way to secrete insulin than to eat foods that either contain sugar or are quickly broken down into sugar. The net result is condition-1 (a rapid rise in sugar concentration). Research shows that eating two slices of bread with jam can raise insulin by 460 percent. That's two measly pieces of jelly bread. Imagine what a binge could do!

Condition-2

What makes a carbohydrate complex? Is it the carbohydrate's love of ballet, Shakespeare, and mud wrestling? I don't think so! When nutritionists speak of complex carbohydrates, they are referring to carbohydrates that retain their natural vitamins, minerals, and fiber. When carbohydrates are processed, they are skinned of these calorie-free gems, leaving behind just a lot of densely packed calories.

Compared to complex carbohydrates, HPCs and sugars are caloric lead weights.

For example, picture ten tiny jelly beans. Combined, they are about the size of your average strawberry. But stuffed into those ten chewy little beans are 25% more calories than an entire jumbo grapefruit. So if you want to consume a lot of calories, and release plenty of insulin cops (condition-2), then HPCs and sugar are the way to do it. After all, which would be easier to binge on, a handful of jelly beans or six jumbo grapefruit? Everyone who said jelly beans, give yourself a Gold Star.

But What about Fats?

Fats are fats. Fats aren't sugar. Not very profound, but true nonetheless. Since fats are not sugar, they obviously don't cause a rapid rise in sugar concentration. Therefore, fats do not fuel condition-1. So then, what's all the fuss about fats and compulsive overeating? Ahh, Good question. The answer is, condition-2.

If HPCs and sugar are caloric lead weights, then fats are caloric plutonium–or something else that's really, really dense (i.e. the politician of your choice). The point is, fats contain more than twice the calories of carbohydrates on a gram for gram basis. One gram of carbohydrate contains 4 calories, but one gram of fat contains 9 of these little buggers. So you see, fatty foods are calorie magnets. If you want to consume several calories at once and send your serotonin levels soaring, then fat is the food for you.

The Foods That Feed

What foods am I talking about? Which ones disrupt serotonin and feed your feelings? For the most part, I'm talking about cakes, pies, cookies, and ice cream–pretty much all the junk food that you know isn't good for you, but simply can't resist. This includes chips, fries, and all the rest of the greasy fatty foods your body craves. But I'm also talking about some foods that may seem healthy. In fact, they probably are healthy for most people, but not for you. I'm talking about bread and pasta.

Think about it. Bread and pasta are really consummate examples of processed carbohydrates. You start with some nice wholesome grain, then pulverize the heck out of it until it's reduced to an amorphous blob of flour. Add some yeast, egg, or maybe a little water, then mash it into dough. Voila! You have oodles of noodles or loads of loaves. Either way, you are left with highly processed carbohydrates that are quickly broken down into sugar the moment they hit your belly. That's sugar that releases insulin, wages war on serotonin, and feeds your feelings.

Feeding your feelings with pasta was no secret to Brenda. She did it for years. "Spaghetti was my anesthesia," she says, "It numbed my nerves whenever I felt stressed." Brenda isn't alone. My guess is, at some point, you too have soothed your sorrows with bread or pasta. After all, medicating your mood with HPCs, sugar, and excess fat is something every compulsive overeater does. But why? To answer this, we'll need to take a quick look at the relationship between serotonin, mood, food, and even...

...PMS

Wow! Talk about an abrupt transition. PMS??? What's this have to do with compulsive overeating? Well, a few pages back, I mentioned that there is a spectrum of illnesses where abnormalities in serotonin play a role (major depression, obsessive-compulsive disorder, alcoholism, etc.). Well here's another one to add to the list: premenstrual syndrome. PMS provides an ideal model for the relationship between serotonin and carbohydrate craving.

For years, PMS was viewed as a neurotic condition. The mood swings, irritability, cramping, bloating, and even the irresistible urges to devour sweets that accompanied "that time of the month" were felt to be merely psychosomatic. But the last decade produced considerable biologic evidence that substantiates women's long held belief–their suffering is real, and not "just in their heads."

PMS isn't a disorder of any single chemical. The menstrual cycle involves an intricate interplay of many body chemicals including pituitary hormones, estrogen, progesterone, and of course, serotonin. Several recent studies demonstrate that in the week prior to menses, women with premenstrual syndrome have markedly lower levels of serotonin than women without PMS. With this reduction in their calming chemical comes much of the discomfort and moodiness that typifies PMS.

Although the symptoms of PMS vary widely from woman to woman, carbohydrate craving seems to be universal. Controlled studies show that women with PMS increase their carbohydrate intake by as much as 500 calories in the three to four days prior to their period. These same women report feeling less depressed and less anxious after eating a meal loaded with carbohydrates. Researchers believe this finding proves the effectiveness of self-medicating with certain foods to manipulate serotonin.

In fact, many nutritionists advise PMS sufferers to eat extra bread, pasta, and sweets in the days prior to menses. These dietary modifications can relieve the transient emotional symptoms of menstrually related serotonin deficiencies. But can you imagine having to eat like that every day just to feel normal? Of course you can. This is your life! This is exactly what you've been doing day, after day, after day.

As a compulsive overeater, you inherited a particularly fragile and persistent serotonin deficiency. But unlike PMS sufferers, you need to compensate for this deficiency with a *continuous* mode of overeating. Your serotonin system is always disrupted. That's why you are constantly driven to binge. On some subconscious level, you learned to boost serotonin by gorging yourself on HPCs, sugar, and excess fat. (Remember the 447% increase in serotonin from just two slices of bread with jam.) The bottom line is that you over-eat in order to medicate the defective serotonin system with which you were born. It's the only way you know to cope with your disease and obtain enough of the calming chemical that the rest of the world takes for granted. But don't be fooled. Compulsive overeating doesn't offer any lasting relief. Eventually comes weight gain, worsening self-esteem, guilt, depression, and ultimately–food failure!

Why Food Fails

I once sent away for a package of sea-monkeys. Maybe you remember seeing them in the back of your favorite childhood magazine. The advertisement was unforgettable. Pour them into a bowl, add water, and soon little sea-monkey boys and girls would spring to life, riding their sea-monkey cycles, having a blast, and guaranteeing you hours of fun. Well, I got my sea-monkey kit, and it was tragic. My sea-monkey children weren't children at all. They were just a bunch of unsightly shrimp larvae that went belly up–fast! The guaranteed hours of fun were just guaranteed hours of scum–sea-monkey scum, that is. I learned a valuable lesson: what you see is definitely not always what you get.

Binge food fools you in a similar way. It offers the promise of an immediate increase in serotonin and a temporary sense of well-being. But the operative word here is *temporary*. Over the long run, compulsive overeating leads to an even greater deficiency in serotonin. Here's why.

HPCs, sugar, and excess fat have a *biphasic effect* on serotonin–sort of like the chemical version of Disney's *Space Mountain*. In the first phase (binge phase) your serotonin coaster climbs higher and higher, until it reaches the pinnacle of excitement–a sense of well-being. Then the true terror of the ride unleashes as your serotonin coaster plunges so far down that it can't make it back to the starting point. Now you feel worse than ever. So you binge again, not only to correct the serotonin deficiency you were born with, but also to counteract the biphasic effect. It's a roller coaster ride that seemingly never ends and you have a front row seat.

How does this happen? How does compulsive overeating eventually cause serotonin levels to nose-dive even further? The answer is not entirely clear. However, we do know that obesity is characterized by a condition called *insulin resistance*. This simply means that the obese individual's insulin cops aren't as effective as they once were (kind of like Barnaby Jones in his last few episodes). When insulin isn't working properly, your body can't convert carbohydrates into energy. Instead, your liver is forced to breakdown amino acids, such as tryptophan, and transform them into the fuel your body needs. As a result, tryptophan that should become serotonin is instead used for energy. The net effect is that serotonin levels plummet.

However, not all compulsive overeaters are insulin resistant. So what else explains serotonin's downward plunge from continued bingeing? One likely candidate is a process called, *the negative feedback loop*. In order to visualize this process, imagine that your job is to place widgets on thing-a-ma-bobs as they roll along a conveyer belt. Suppose one day, a gazillion thing-a-ma-bobs come barreling down the assembly line all at once. You think to yourself, "This must be some kind of horrible mistake. If a gazillion thing-a-ma-bobs and widgets were to fall into the wrong hands, it would upset the very balance of world power." So being the quick thinker that you are, you hit the factory's emergency stop button, halt production, save mankind, and then head straight for a coffee break—you're a Teamster!

Your body is a pretty darn sophisticated factory. Emergency stop buttons exist for several metabolic activities. Of course now that we are talking about the body, we have to start using unnecessarily complicated words. So we no longer call it an emergency stop button, but rather a negative feedback loop. The principle is the same. Your body halts production of a chemical once it senses that enough already exists.

HPCs, sugar, and excess fat may fool your system by producing a burst of serotonin that mistakenly tells your body,

"Hey, too much serotonin is already here, so shutdown the factory." By the time your body realizes that it's just a false alarm, it's too late. You have already punched your time card and gone home for the day. Again, the end result is another decrease in serotonin, another worsening of your mood, and another reason to binge!

Stressed to Kill

She died of a broken heart. He worried himself sick. She aged so quickly since her retirement. Of course he had a heart attack, he's a workaholic. We've all heard variations of these statements. Stress makes people ill. It's just common sense.

Scientists, however, never take common sense at face value. They must study, analyze, and test common sense to see if it is really true. But before they even do this, they must first give a name to their common sense theory that's utterly incomprehensible. Hence the birth of the *stress diatheses* model of illness. After twelve years of post high school education, I still had to crack open Webster's and look up "diatheses."

The stress diatheses model is an even fancier name for the two-hit hypothesis. It presumes that people have certain vulnerabilities (diatheses) that when stressed, produce illness. Unfortunately, this appears to be especially true for you. In fact, recent research suggests that stress can chemically compel you to do the one thing you dread most. BINGE!

I Can't Believe I Ate the Whole Thing!

Just when you thought it was safe to keep reading without stumbling over more techno-babble, let me toss these two verbal hurdles in your way: *Dynorphin* and *Beta-Endorphin*. These are your body's "feel-good" chemicals. Your brain releases them when you feel stressed. They produce feelings of pleasure that make stressful situations far more bearable.

In fact, they work so well they create a *positive feedback loop* that drives you to binge.

If the negative feedback loop acts as your body's emergency stop button, then the positive feedback loop is definitely your Yipee, Yipee–Yes...YES...**YES** button. It feels so good to push, you just keep pushing it. Unfortunately, the button you are pushing is food. Here's how it works.

When you are stressed, your brain releases dynorphin. Dynorphin causes you to crave and eat sweet, carbohydrate-rich foods. HPCs and sugar then stimulate the release of beta-endorphin. Beta-endorphin gives you a sensation of pleasure–Yipee! But unbeknownst to you, it too causes you to crave and eat sweets. So what do you do? You eat more HPCs and sugar, and release more beta-endorphin–Yahoo, feelin' good now! But the more beta-endorphin you release, the more you are driven to eat. The loop seems endless. You eat and eat, producing more and more beta-endorphin. The beta-endorphin reduces your immediate stress, but also propels you to binge. Eventually, you binge until you are stuffed.

Now the irony begins. You just gorged yourself to relieve stress. Are you proud of yourself? No! You feel guilty for losing control, worthless because you've done this so many times before, and hopeless because you know it's going to happen again. Are these happy thoughts? No, they are stressful thoughts, and what happens when you're stressed? Dynorphin is released and you start craving HPCs and sugar again. Aaaaaarrrgh! Welcome to the "positive" feedback loop. Not much positive about it, eh?

Opioids Anonymous

Dynorphin and beta-endorphin are two very attractive chemicals that your brain just loves. So why do they always get the best of you? Why is the cycle they create so difficult to break? The answer lies not so much in their chemical reaction, but in their chemical attraction.

Dynorphin and beta-endorphin are both members of a

family of chemicals called *opioids*. Like serotonin, opioids are one of your body's chemical communicators. But that's where the similarities end. Because structurally, opioids have nothing in common with serotonin. In fact, the chemical that opioids resemble most, in both design and action, is heroin.

Yes, opioids are your body's narcotic fix for what ails you. They are your own private poppy field. The "runner's high" that joggers experience isn't from a mystical connection between man and his Reeboks. It's from opioids. That's why every now and then, clients will tell me that they can stop cravings by exercising rigorously. They think they can burn the cravings right out of their systems, but actually they've found just another way to manipulate their opioids.

Don't get me wrong, opioids are normal, natural, God-given defenses against pain and stress. But many experts believe that certain behaviors manipulate opioids so effectively that they become downright habit forming. Bingeing is a perfect example. Which kind of makes you wonder. Is compulsive overeating more than a disease? Is it an addiction?

Chapter 3

Food Addiction: Fact or Fiction

The Great Debate

Want to create controversy with just two words? Try these two: *Food Addiction*. For many, the notion of being physically hooked on junk food is preposterous. Physicians are often the biggest cynics; most view food addiction as just another lame excuse for a lack of willpower. I've even overheard several fellow psychiatrists sarcastically comment, "Yeah, I guess I'm a food addict too. If I don't eat, I'll die."

Despite such rampant skepticism, there's a growing movement to view compulsive overeating as an addictive illness similar to alcoholism or drug abuse. Twelve-step recovery programs like Overeaters Anonymous, and books such as *Food Addiction, The Body Knows* and *The Carbohydrate Addicts Diet* are now quite popular.

Feel free to "boo" and "hiss," but I initially entered this

heated debate siding with the skeptics and naysayers. Boooo! Hissss! Sorry, but I too was convinced that food addiction was about as real as the Tooth Fairy. Well, I was wrong. Food addiction is the real deal. Trust me. Of course I understand if you aren't ready to take this leap of faith, but at least consider this one question: *Is food a drug?*

An Apple a Day...

...Keeps the doctor away. Who told you this? Parents, doctors, teachers–the same people who said, "Milk, it does a body good," or "Finish your juice so you don't catch a cold." The very same people who now look at you, shake their heads at your ignorance, and say, "Oh no no no. Food addiction, don't be silly. Food isn't a drug."

Of course food is a drug, especially carbohydrates. It's ridiculous to argue otherwise. After all, most modern medications are derived from plant life. The last time I checked, wheat, sugar cane, fruits, and veggies–all the good places that carbohydrates come from–are PLANTS! I never once saw Marlin Perkins stalking a mango or cucumber on *Wild Kingdom*. Have you? Okay, that settles it. Drugs come from plants. Plants are food. Food is a drug–Yikes, it's that transitive property of addition rule I learned in grade school.

Hopefully, my incessant yapping about serotonin and endorphin has already convinced you that food can be a drug. If not, I'll spare you the agony of repeating myself; but if you are still doubting me, then please reconsider these four facts:

1. HPCs and sugar are processed foods.
2. HPCs and sugar, especially when combined with fat, cause serotonin and endorphin levels in the brain to skyrocket.
3. Both serotonin and endorphin regulate emotion.
4. For compulsive overeaters, HPCs, sugar, and excess fat act as drugs to medicate a poorly functioning serotonin-emotion system.

Are you swayed? Are you putty in my hands? Are you a food addiction convert? Not even close, huh. You're saying to yourself, "A drug is one thing, but an addiction—who does this doofus think he's kidding?"

You have a right to be skeptical. I suppose I have made it seem as though you can pick an ear of corn, taste it, and suddenly become a Birdseye addict. Obviously that's not true, but I'm not talking about corn. I'm talking about binge food; and something happens in the transition from whole kernel corn-on-the-cob to the bag of Fritos sitting in your cupboard—something called PROCESSING.

Processing chemicals to make them more addictive is seen time and time again in the study of chemical dependency. For example, cocaine begins with the *Erythroxylon coca* plant. Its leaves contain approximately 1% cocaine. Soak the leaves, mash them, turn them into a paste, extract the juice, then clarify it with hydrochloric acid. In other words, process it! What do you get? Mounds of pure white crystalline cocaine.

Sugar follows a similar pathway. Start with the *Saccharum officinarium* plant. Its sap contains approximately 13% sugar. Soak it, mash it, turn it into molasses, extract the juice, then clarify it with phosphoric acid. In other words, process it! Now what do you get? A completely different white crystal—sugar!

The comparison of coca to cocaine, cane to sugar, poppy to heroin, or whole wheat to flour, can just as easily be made for any addictive substance. Processing increases potency.

Are you still doubting? Maybe. Maybe not. You see, the above analogy is somewhat misleading. Yes, addictive drugs are processed, but so are most medications. Your doctor doesn't say, "Here, take this twig and call me in the morning," does he? Of course not. He or she gives you a pill that has been processed. Processing increases potency, but that doesn't necessarily equate to addiction. Antibiotics are processed, but I don't know of any Colombian penicillin cartels!

So what really separates addictive drugs from purely medicinal ones? It's not a matter of plant versus animal, or processed versus whole food. It's not even a matter of being able to alter emotion—antidepressants do that and they certainly aren't addictive. What really makes a drug addictive is its potential to create dependence: *a drug seeking drive so powerful that the ensuing social, emotional, and physical consequences are completely disregarded.* If food addiction is to be accepted as a bonafide disease, then evidence of clinical dependency must be demonstrated.

My Name is Leann and I'm a Chocoholic

"Just once I'd like to meet a man who excites
me as much as a Snickers bar."
- *Leann*

That's how Leann introduced herself during our first session; and despite her success at breaking the ice, the poignancy of Leann's remark rang hauntingly true. Chocolate controlled her. From the five Snickers she ate each day, to her sweat shirt that read, "Hand over the candy and no one gets hurt," Leann symbolized the essence of *chocoholism.*

Leann used her sense of humor to mask her inner pain; but in reality, Leann's life was in a tailspin. Compulsive overeating interfered with her health, work, and relationships. Leann was absolutely certain she was hooked on binge food; so I put her conviction to the test by looking in a book called the DSM-IV.

The Diagnostic and Statistical Manual of Mental Disorders (DSM-IV) defines the manifestations of every conceivable emotional illness. Buried within its 886 pages are the diagnostic criterion for substance dependence. If you really want to put the concept of food addiction to the test, then determining if compulsive overeaters meet the DSM-IV's strict criterion is essential. With this in mind, let's look at the DSM-IV criterion for substance dependence and compare them with Leann's experiences.

DSM-IV Criteria for Substance Dependence

A maladaptive pattern of substance use, leading to clinically significant impairment or distress, as manifested by *three* (or more) of the following, occurring at any time in the same 12-month period:

DSM-IV	Leann's Responses
1. tolerance, as defined by either of the following: (a) a need for markedly increased amounts of the substance to achieve intoxication or the desired effect (b) markedly diminished effect with continued use of the same amount of substance	"I used to think that bingeing on half a loaf of bread was insane, but lately I've been eating an entire loaf in just one sitting."
2. withdrawal, as manifested by either of the following: (a) characteristic withdrawal symptoms (b) substance is taken to relieve or avoid withdrawal symptoms	"I used to try a different diet every week. By the third or fourth day, my hunger-headache and irritability were so bad that I would binge just to relieve the pain."
3. the substance is often taken in larger amounts or over a longer period of time than was intended	"I planned to eat just one scoop of ice cream, but I wound up eating the whole half gallon."
4. there is a persistent desire or unsuccessful efforts to cut down or control substance use	"I think I've tried every diet ever invented, but I always wound up heavier than when I started."
5. a great deal of time is spent in activities necessary to obtain the substance, or recover from its effects	"I guess it's pretty bad when the cashiers at Dairy Queen know you by name."
6. important social, occupational, or recreational activities given up or reduced because of substance use	"I eventually lost my job as an aide to the elderly because I was caught stealing food. I even turned down a date once because I had just baked some cookies and wanted to eat them while they were still hot."
7. the substance use is continued despite knowledge of having a persistent or recurrent social, psychological, or physical problem that is caused or exacerbated by the use of the substance	"I have asthma. I used to eat so fast that I would get short of breath and have to use my inhaler between bites."

Is Leann a food addict? You betcha! While she only needed to meet three of the DSM-IV criterion to satisfy the requirements for substance dependence, Leann met each and every one. How many criterion do you meet? Three? Five? All seven? How many times have you said to yourself, "Just one more bite," to be followed by another, and another, and another? How many times have you fallen off the diet wagon? How many blows to your ego, self esteem, and health has bingeing cost you? Most compulsive overeaters easily meet the DSM-IV criterion. Do you?

Savings and Withdrawal

I like payday. I walk to the bank, hand my check to the teller, and smile as she stamps the new deposit in my passbook. Yes, saving money warms my heart. But then, as they say, "IT happens." Oh, there's a different IT every week, but there is always an IT. IT can be a broken water heater. IT can be a flat tire. IT can even be my wife's birthday—that's a really big IT. IT makes me go to the bank, take out my pretty money, and give it to someone else. Ouch! My once warm heart begins to ache. IT hurts! For compulsive overeaters, binge food is a lot like my savings. It feels good going in, but withdrawal is a painful experience.

One tormentingly obvious argument that compulsive overeating is indeed an addiction is *withdrawal*. You've probably experienced withdrawal before. It's the crummy feeling you had around day three of every diet. You felt irritable, tired, headachy, and maybe even dizzy or nauseous; but you knew you would feel much better if you just had a taste of something sweet. That's withdrawal—your brain adapting to life without sugary highs.

There's no way around withdrawal. You just have to plunge straight through it. The flu-like symptoms you might experience won't last more than a few days, so don't try to stave them off by snacking. It only prolongs the agony. Just experience withdrawal, hate it, and swear you'll never go through it again.

The Missing Link

Let's review. Can food be a drug? Yes. Can you become dependent on that drug? Yes. Can you even suffer withdrawal when you stop taking the drug? Yes. Can you finally believe in food addiction??? I hope so, but I imagine there are still a few doubters lurking about. Doubters who say, "Unless you can show me a definite biological connection between compulsive overeating and chemical dependency, I'll never believe in food addiction." Well fasten your seatbelts, here comes serotonin racing to my rescue.

Why do alcoholics drink? That riddle has remained unanswered for years. Recently, however, researchers discovered a major piece to this elusive puzzle. There appears to be a sizable group of alcoholics, who when sober, have a deficiency in–oh you know what I'm going to say–serotonin! That's right. Their nonintoxicated level of this calming chemical is low. What happens when they binge on alcohol? They get a giant boost in serotonin. That's really no surprise, considering alcohol is nothing more than highly processed liquid sugar.

Scientists now believe that alcohol's ability to boost serotonin can be profoundly rewarding. In fact, from a chemical standpoint, some alcoholics may feel normal only when intoxicated. Sound familiar? It should. These alcoholics seem to self-medicate with booze, the same way you use HPCs, sugar, and excess fat. Same serotonin defect. Same behavior. Same addiction. Just a different drug!

I'll be the first to admit it. I'm no Perry Mason, but haven't I done a good job of proving my case? Compulsive overeating is an addiction, not a weakness.

So tell me. Are you ready to encourage controversy? Are you ready to stand up to the doubters? Are you ready to thumb your nose at your friends, family, and ninety percent of the medical community? If so, then recite with me the compulsive overeater's adaptation of the Tinkerbell Oath: "I do believe–I do believe–I do believe in Food Addiction!"

Chapter 4

The Physical Costs of Compulsive Overeating

Opposites Attract

Jan and Billy were so physically different, it seemed impossible that they could coexist in the same gravity. Yet there they were, sitting in my waiting room one Saturday morning chatting like old friends. The visual impression they cast was unforgettable.

Jan was nearly six feet tall yet weighed less than one hundred thirty pounds. Long blonde hair cascaded over her face, camouflaging weathered brown eyes. At twenty-three, Jan was going on forty.

Ralph, in contrast, was just shy of 5'8" and almost as wide. Four hundred twenty-seven pounds of flesh supported a boyish face and devilish grin that gave no hint of his true age, fifty-three.

As the two stood to introduce themselves, with tall, thin Jan standing to my left, and short, round Billy standing to my right, their silhouettes combined to form the shadowy embodiment of the number **10**.

What strange rift in the space-time continuum accounted for their mutual presence at my door step? Was it a black hole, perhaps? How about a super nova? Maybe a cosmic string? Nope, no such luck! Actually, it was a far less celestial force. A force named Dr. Robert Manning.

Dr. Bob, as he liked to be called, was the local throat specialist. It turned out that he recently performed surgery on both Jan and Billy, and the two patients became pals during their postoperative recovery. But their friendship was far deeper than you would expect, especially for two people who just happened to be in the same place at the same time.

It's said that tragedy shared can bring even strangers together. So perhaps it was Jan and Billy's close brush with death that truly forged their kinship. It was certainly what prompted Dr. Bob to refer them to me.

Jan's Story

Jan had a long history of bulimia. Like many bulimics, she had several ritualistic eating behaviors. This one nearly killed her:

> Once a day, for the last three years, I devoured a small loaf of bread and a pound of pasta. I would scarf down the noodles so fast that I barely chewed twice before swallowing. Then, just as quickly, I would force myself to drink three full glasses of water to prepare my meal for its round trip journey. As soon as I finished the water, I would enter the bathroom, stick my finger down my throat, and vomit.

Jan's habitual purging gradually dilated, weakened, and thinned the walls of her esophagus so badly that one day, during the throes of her bulimic ritual, Jan's esophagus had a "blowout" and ruptured. The ambulance rushed to the scene just as she went into shock. By the time Jan arrived at the hospital, her condition was critical. Dr. Bob performed emergency surgery to stop the internal bleeding and repair the damage. The surgery was a success, but Jan developed a nasty postoperative infection and spent ten extra days in intensive care.

The consequences of compulsive overeating took Jan by surprise. Within seconds, her life drastically changed. In comparison, the consequences of Billy's overeating were far more insidious.

Billy's Story

Billy began gaining weight at age fourteen, shortly after the death of his father. At the funeral, Billy's mom chastised him for crying. "Billy," she demanded, "Put a smile on your face and stop all that blubbering. You're the man of the family now, so act like it." Since then, Billy never spilled a tear nor raised his voice. Instead, he became a master of illusion, learning to maintain a bright, happy facade no matter how sad and lonely he truly felt. Covering up his feelings wasn't easy, but stuffing them down with food seemed to help. Half a box of Ho-Hos usually did the trick. If that failed, he just kept eating until the pain from his ensuing stomachache displaced all his sorrow.

Billy's weight soared exponentially. By his 30th birthday, he was well over 300 pounds, his blood pressure was skyrocketing, and arthritis began to cripple his knees. At 40, he felt completely drained of energy and couldn't concentrate. To make matters worse, he began drifting off to sleep on the subway.

Okay, so maybe sleeping on the subway isn't such a big deal. One major problem though—Billy was the conductor. Catnapping at the wheel was considered bad form. So why was Billy so sleepy? Because he developed *obstructive sleep apnea.*

Apnea, is Latin for "without breath." Obstructive sleep apnea refers to any condition in which a blockage interrupts breathing during sleep. In Billy's case, the obstruction was the shear girth of his neck and throat. When Billy drifted off to dreamland, the muscles of his throat relaxed and the weight of his massive neck crushed his airway shut.

With Billy's airway tightly sealed, there was no way for oxygen to get into his lungs. This didn't make Billy's lungs happy. So Mr. and Mrs. Lung gave Billy two choices: wake up and breathe, or die! Given those options, the decision was easy. Billy was forced to wake up several times each night and gasp for air, leaving him tired, sluggish, and asleep at the wheel.

Billy's wife still recalls the terror she felt the first time she witnessed an episode of his apnea:

> He was snoring away as usual and then all of a sudden, nothing–complete silence–no movement. I thought he was dead! But before I could react, he made the loudest SNORT I ever heard, woke up briefly, and then went right back to sawing logs. He had twenty more of those spells that night. Each one lasted about half a minute. Maybe he slept some that night, but I sure didn't. I dragged him to the doctor's office the next day. The doctor said Billy had apnea and then prescribed the most conservative therapy he knew–weight loss!

Billy tried to follow his doctor's advise. Effort after effort met with initial success but ultimately ended in failure. His weight was 350, then 360...370...380 and so on, until Billy weighed more than 420 pounds. Each new pound made breathing and sleeping increasingly more difficult. As a result, Billy grew too tired to exert any effort to exercise. Without exercise, his metabolism slowed even further. Billy was caught in a trap that made weight loss impossible. His spells of apnea began to lengthen. Billy's wife noticed that his breathing was stopping for close to a minute at a time. Once again, she dragged him back to the doctor, but this time, conservative treatment wasn't an option. Billy's condition had worsened, his health was diminishing, and heart failure was just around the corner. Dr. Bob was consulted.

Dr. Bob realized that in such a severe case of obstructive sleep apnea, the current standard of medical care called for an—are you ready for this one—Uvulopalatopharyngoplasty. What in the name of all things that are long and unpronounceable is an Uvulopalatopharyngoplasty? Simply stated, it is a surgical procedure that removes the little thing that dangles down the back of your throat when you say AAH, as well as the tissue that surrounds it. Scooping out these structures is like hollowing out the core of a pumpkin. It widens the airway and helps oxygen flow.

Believe it or not, this procedure isn't typically considered major surgery. But Billy was no typical guy. His high blood pressure, diabetes, and obesity all added to the usual operative risks. Although Billy's surgery was successful, his recovery was slow, and his hospital stay nearly twice as long as anticipated. Fortunately, the time Billy spent recuperating allowed him to reflect upon the consequences of his compulsive overeating and to make the acquaintance of his new friend, Jan.

Obesity

If you were roaming the barren dunes of the Sahara, maybe you wouldn't mind wearing a nice thick layer of fat. It might keep you from starving on the slim pickings of desert life. But I doubt you are living in the wild, so there's really no reason to store fat like a camel does in its hump. Nevertheless, 34 million Americans are doing just that. Today, more than 1 out of 5 adults are overweight. Even with the latest fitness craze, the incidence of overeating and obesity continues to rise.

To be fair, overeating is not the sole basis of obesity. The proverbial "glandular problems" and "slow metabolisms" do indeed exist, but they are rare. Quite frankly, most obesity

is the result of too much food in and not enough energy out.
Irrespective of the cause, obesity is a time bomb waiting
to explode. The Surgeon General's Report notes that even a
few extra pounds can increase the risk of premature death.
Among the medical consequences of obesity that lead to this
increased mortality are:

Diabetes: Eighty to ninety percent of adult onset
diabetics are obese. Untreated diabetes is the leading cause of adult blindness in this country. Diabetics are also at a substantially greater risk for circulatory disease, kidney failure, progressive nervous
system dysfunction, and infection. Very often, weight
loss is all that is needed to treat this form of diabetes.

Heart and Circulatory Disease: Obesity is a risk
factor for developing high blood pressure, hardening
of the arteries, and elevated triglyceride levels. Independently, any one of these can significantly increase
the likelihood of a heart attack or stroke. Combine
them, and the certainty of cardiovascular harm
multiplies.

Respiratory Disease: Obesity results from an en-
largement of existing fat cells rather than the production of new fatty tissue. As fat cells grow larger,
they thicken the tissue surrounding the throat and
obstruct breathing. This creates periodic interrup-
tions in the supply of oxygen to the lungs. In severe
cases, such disruptions can lead to fatigue, conges-
tive heart failure, and according to the experts, sudden death. (Billy the Kid once shot a man simply for
snoring too loudly—but I don't think this is the kind
of sudden death the experts are implying.)

Gallbladder Disease: Eight billion dollars are
spent each year on the treatment of gallbladder disease. Thirty percent of these costs are attributed to

obesity. The obese food addict is twice as likely as their normal weight counterpart to suffer the agonizing abdominal pain induced by gall stones. Removing the inflamed organ is normally a routine procedure, but can be life threatening if a patient is overweight.

Musculoskeletal Disease: Muscles and bones were not designed to endure the forces of excess weight. Obesity places the weight-bearing joints, like the hips and knees, in jeopardy of developing severe degenerative arthritis. Likewise, chronic back and foot disease are frequently worsened by weight gain.

Cancer: Several forms of cancer are linked to obesity. In overweight women, cancer of the breast, uterus, ovaries, and gallbladder are more likely to occur. Similarly, obese men are prone to develop cancer of the prostate, rectum, and colon.

Many other conditions are induced or aggravated by obesity including: menstrual irregularities, hernias, gout, and varicose veins. A recent survey estimated that the yearly financial toll of diabetes, hypertension, heart and gallbladder disease, as well as breast and colon cancer directly attributed to obesity was $39.3 billion. That's $1,155 per year spent on each obese individual just to cover the health related expenses of a few illnesses. Amazingly, if all the physical consequences of both bingeing and purging were included in this forecast, the actual yearly expense would likely double or triple.

Bulimia

"I eat like a cow." That's how Molly describes her insatiable appetite. Her choice of metaphor is uncannily accurate. You see, Molly is bulimic; and the word *bulimia* comes from two Greek words meaning "ox" and "hunger." Of course it takes far more than gluttony to consider Molly a bulimic. She also has an obsessive preoccupation with her body and feels terribly out of control whenever she eats. So far, Molly sounds like your run-of-the-mill compulsive overeater, doesn't she? But the kicker for Molly, and for all bulimics, is the drastic measures she takes to lose weight. She throws-up, abuses laxatives, and over-exercises to exhaustion. Molly has a problem; she's a compulsive overeater who decided to purge.

Purging seems like such a senseless choice. "Why bother?" you ask. Molly's answer appears to ring true for all bulimics, "I honestly thought it was the only way I could lose weight, and I'd do ANYTHING to be thin." And so begins the next perilous twist in the spiral of compulsive overeating.

No compulsive overeater starts out bulimic. It is an evolutionary process. First you binge. Then you gain weight. Next you feel shame toward your loss of self-control. Then shame turns to fear—a fear of perpetual weight gain. Finally, fear turns into desperation; and desperation leads to purging. But the food addict's belief that purging is a great way to lose weight is no different than the alcoholic's belief that coffee is a great way to sober up. Both convictions are dead wrong.

Most eating disorder specialists believe self-induced vomiting is actually habit forming and encourages overeating. "How?" you ask. Simply because patients mistakenly think that by vomiting they will avoid absorbing what they eat. Consequently, bulimics tend to relax their dietary controls and actually binge more frequently. Molly identifies with most of this concept but disagrees with the last part. She says:

> I never had control of my diet to begin with. I thought making myself throw up might actually bring some order back into my life. But eventually even that got out of hand. Now I throw up after every meal, even

after eating just a piece of fruit. I don't get it! I should be starving to death, yet somehow I don't seem to lose much weight.

Molly's bewilderment stems from the common misunderstanding that vomiting ejects the entire contents of the stomach. It does not! Self-induced vomiting retrieves only a portion of what you eat. Since most binges involve several thousand calories, enough food can easily be absorbed to further weight gain despite vomiting.

Other methods of purging arise from similar misconceptions. For example, laxatives and diuretics will help you lose weight—right? Wrong! Laxatives have very little effect (and diuretics have none) on the absorption of calories. In essence, all they remove is vital and "calorie-free" water. Likewise, most physicians agree that unsupervised fasting is unhealthy and almost always induces an enormous binge.

The oasis of benefits reaped by purging is a mirage. In truth, bulimia is a crime against self. As with any crime, the degree of punishment varies with the maliciousness of the act. Take a look at what the crimes of purging can do to you.

Misdemeanors: These are the least offensive crimes of purging; but like other misdemeanors, they are often the most distressing. Take vandalism for example. There's no real physical harm done. It's just a simple property crime. Nevertheless, such willful destruction can permanently ruin the beauty of something that was once quite lovely.

Bulimics vandalize their own appearance each and every time they purge. Vomit bathes the bulimic's mouth with stomach acids that corrode teeth and strip them of their enamel. Stained, cavity-filled teeth are the unsightly results. Also, since most bulimics make themselves throw up by sticking their fingers down their throat, painfully visible calluses and ulcers often form on their hands.

Other aesthetic problems arising from bulimia include dry skin, rashes, pimples, as well as swollen hands and feet. These cosmetic repercussions deliver a devastating blow to a self-image that is already quite distorted.

Felonies: These are far more serious crimes than misdemeanors. Purging is a felonious form of assault that is capable of inflicting substantial injury to its victim—the bulimic.

Excessive vomiting batters the bulimic, leading to hernias, infected salivary glands, and even seizures. On other occasions, vomit can accidentally get sucked into the lungs and evolve into a life threatening pneumonia.

Laxatives assail the bulimic's health in far more embarrassing, but equally dangerous ways. Laxative abuse can create a physical dependency so severe, that bowel movements can not occur without them. Worse yet, some bulimics lose control of their bowels altogether and need to wear diapers. At a minimum, laxative abuse promotes cramps and anal irritation.

Other complications arising from purging include dehydration, kidney failure, and muscle spasms. You would think that suffering the consequences of just one of these crimes would deter any further bulimic felonies. Alas, most bulimics are repeat offenders.

Capital Offenses: Murder is a heinous crime. One for which the most finite of punishments is reserved —the death sentence. A rare yet real penalty of purging is a self-imposed execution in which the bulimic becomes victim, perpetrator, and assassin all rolled into one.

The forcefulness of habitual vomiting can weaken, tear, and occasionally rupture the walls of the stomach or esophagus. This can lead to hemorrhage, infection, and in extreme cases, an agonizing death. Minor abdominal pain may be the only warning sign of this catastrophic demise.

However, most bulimics who die as a result of

purging do so without any warning at all. Sudden cardiac death is the leading killer of bulimics. Purging removes potassium, a mineral that's crucial to proper cardiac function. Without enough potassium, the heart's internal pacemaker can short circuit and end life abruptly.

Likewise, Serum of Ipecac, a drug taken by many bulimics to induce vomiting, is particularly toxic to the heart. It likely contributed to the death of singer, Karen Carpenter.

The "no pain no gain" mentality of today's society encourages the bulimic's destructive march toward vanity. Yet when the smoke clears and the dust settles, the rewards of purging are illusory, while the physical penalties are very substantial.

Wading Through Denial

Dr. Bob did much more than restore Jan and Billy's physical health. He rescued their spirits as well. Along with Jan's esophagus and Billy's uvula, Dr. Bob removed the last vestiges of their denial. Denial that clouded recognition of their illnesses and blocked all hope for recovery. Denial that boasted, "It can't happen to you. You're too young, too smart, too healthy." Denial that preached the false mantra, "You're in control," as their lives became more unmanageable. Denial that nearly killed them.

Jan and Billy's sagas are not unique. Denial whispers deceit into the ears of all addicts. Compulsive overeaters are no exception. Are you ready to look inward and recognize the consequences of your overeating? Or like Jan and Billy, will you wait for the blinders of denial to be violently ripped from your eyes?

Chances are your esophagus will never explode, and I doubt you'll get so heavy that you suffocate yourself. But take a moment and ask yourself, "Has compulsive overeating jeopardized my health? Am I less energetic? Do I get winded climbing a flight of stairs? Has my doctor advised me to lose weight?" The possibilities are endless, but if you've been honest, your answer must be a resounding, "YES!" Compulsive overeating has taken it's physical toll on you.

Remember, **recognition** is the first step in breaking the **R.U.T.** of compulsive overeating. By recognizing the harmful consequences of bingeing, you've taken more than just a single step. You've taken a Neil Armstrong-like leap toward managing compulsive overeating.

Chapter 5

Depression:
The Sugar Blues

Calamity Jane

Jane tipped the scales at two hundred forty-five pounds the day she tried to take her life. As it turned out, the razor's sharp edge made only a superficial scratch across her wrists. The emergency room doctor called it a suicidal gesture and referred her to a psychiatrist. But to Jane, this was no gesture. She felt hopeless, lost, and out of control. "Two hundred forty-five pounds," she wondered, "How could this be? I've never weighed this much before. Life sucks!"

Jane wasn't always so gloomy. In fact, only eight short months ago she was celebrating a new job, a new beau, and a new diet that reduced her weight all the way down to one hundred sixty-seven pounds. All in all, things seemed great. Then one fateful day, Jane left work early to surprise her boyfriend at his apartment. Unfortunately, the surprise was hers, as she unlocked the door and discovered her boyfriend in bed with another woman. It may seem odd, but Jane didn't say a word. She simply turned around and walked out the door.

Jane wandered the streets for hours before snapping out of her daze. When her fog finally cleared, she found herself standing right in the middle of the snack food isle at her local market. She spent fifteen dollars on junk food that day and finished it all by dusk. Jane's diet was broken along with her heart.

As the next eight months unfolded, so did Jane's life. Bingeing, cravings, weight gain–her entire addictive cycle resurfaced. She became a recluse, sequestered in her bedroom. What little energy she still possessed carried her no further than her kitchen. There, she devoured box after box of pasta. As her weight increased, her sadness deepened and her cravings grew more intense. Never before had Jane felt so hopeless and lost.

Jane's act was no suicidal gesture. She desperately wanted to die. Jane viewed her inability to successfully commit suicide as just another one of her failings–failing diets, failing willpower, and failing health. Oh how she prayed each night not to wake up. Jane had reached the depths of despair. Her compulsive overeating had spiraled out of control and into a full blown major depression.

Some Depressing News

Jane isn't alone. Compulsive overeating is a progressive illness that all too often evolves into true major depression. Unfortunately, friends, family, and even those afflicted are quick to minimize this illness. I can't tell you how many times I've heard compulsive overeaters completely discount their grief with offhanded remarks like, "Of course I'm depressed. Just look at me. I'm hideous! But if I could just lose a few pounds, I'm sure I would feel much better. It's only natural." Well I'm here to tell you that major depression isn't natural and should never be taken lightly. In fact, the only thing "natural" about major depression is the nature of biology itself: faulty genes, faulty chemicals, and faulty neurotransmitters like serotonin.

As you recall, serotonin dysfunction can present itself in several different ways including: compulsive overeating, alcoholism, panic disorder, PMS, and so on. Despite this diversity, it appears that over time these disorders have a tendency to funnel downward into one final pathway–the pathway to major depression.

Nature provides us with several examples of this funneling effect. Atherosclerosis, or "hardening of the arteries," is one such scenario. The early symptoms of this disease are quite varied. Some people develop high blood pressure, while others get leg cramps. Still others experience a temporary weakness in their arms or mouth. Eventually, however, progressive hardening of the arteries is likely to funnel downward into one cataclysmic finale, a massive heart attack. Major depression is the cardiac arrest of the compulsive overeater's serotonin system. It's just as debilitating, just as painful, and often just as deadly.

It is estimated that 17% of all compulsive overeaters attempt suicide at some point in their lives. Countless others are obsessed with wishes to die, but are too despondent to act upon their desires. If allowed to progress, nearly half of all compulsive overeaters become overwhelmed by feelings of worthlessness, hopelessness, and despair–major depression thrown on top of an eating disorder. That's an emotional double jeopardy that leaves its victims with no alternative but to helplessly shake their heads and ask...

...Why Me?

Why are you treading down this pathway toward depression? Well, as my Grandfather used to say, "In the horse race of life, you've won the trifecta of bad luck."

I'm not sure why he said that or what he even meant; but in your case, I think I understand his intentions. Through no fault of your own, you saddled up three ponies that are on the fast track to major depression: Altered Biology, Altered Psychology, and Altered Social Expressivity. Let's take a closer look at this unhealthy trifecta.

Altered Biology

Somewhere in your heritage, major depression lies in ambush. You might guess that the most common emotional illness among family members of compulsive overeaters is another eating disorder. That would be a good guess, but a wrong one. It's major depression. Depression is passed along from generation to generation like an ancient gypsy curse. Not everyone will get it. Heck, it may even skip a decade or two. But sooner or later it will rear its ugly head. Now if your own family is at a heightened risk for depression, then it's no surprise that you are too.

But the biology of major depression doesn't stop at the genetic level. It works its way into your chemistry as well. In fact, the current focus of most biological theories on depression is serotonin, the same chemical wonder that drives you to binge. So it's really no surprise that as each binge wreaks more and more havoc on your serotonin system, another step is taken down the pathway to depression.

Altered Psychology

Sometimes biology can seem so straight forward. There are specific chemicals, specific symptoms, and specific solutions. Psychology, on the other hand, is never an exact science. There just aren't any common emotional tragedies that propel compulsive overeaters toward despondency. There are, however, two well accepted psychological theories on depression that seem particularly applicable to compulsive overeaters: the *Learned Helplessness* and *Cognitive* theories of major depression.

Learned helplessness takes place when you are trapped

in a lousy situation with no foreseeable escape–picture an emotional traffic jam with no exit ramps. Without hope for escape, you eventually learn to be helpless and surrender to fate. You quit honking your horn, stop giving creative hand gestures, and just stare vacantly through the windshield while Captain and Tenile songs play over and over on your AM radio. Not a pretty picture, eh?

Well, failure after failure to break free from compulsive overeating creates a similar state of learned helplessness. Like Jane, most untreated overeaters finally reach a point where they simply give up the fight and surrender to depression.

The cognitive theory views depression from a completely different perspective. According to this theory, depression occurs when you repeatedly think of yourself in a distorted and negative way. Discouraging thoughts like, "I'm worthless, I'm bad, I'm disgusting," are the norm, and pessimism abounds. What compulsive overeater hasn't had these thoughts? All have. But misplaced belief in these distorted impressions will ruin your self-esteem, and leave yet another footprint on the pathway to depression.

Altered Social Expressivity

Altered social expressivity–now there's a mouthful. So just what is it? It's the driving force behind the *Interpersonal* theory of depression. Yes, there are more theories on depression than hairdos in a Dennis Rodman scrapbook. This theory points out that most episodes of depression begin during times of troubled personal relationships (social) and poor feelings management (expressivity). Look at Jane. Her depression began shortly after her romance collapsed; leaving her too paralyzed to express her feelings toward the big jerk who cheated on her. Instead, she stuffed them down deep in her belly–a bite of fear, a morsel of loneliness, and a spoonful of anger. That's what feeding your feelings is all about–mismanaging feelings through bingeing, until only one negative feeling remains–DEPRESSION!

The Great Depression

15 million! That's how many Americans will experience major depression. Sadly, 85% of them will be too frightened or misinformed to seek treatment. That's a shocking number of people resigned to spending much of their existence needlessly wallowing in misery.

It isn't easy acknowledging that the fabric of our psyche is vulnerable to emotional disorders. Perhaps that's why society has long perpetuated the stigma of mental illness as a "personal weakness." Such illusions create a false sense of security. We sleep easier at night believing the anguish of others stems from their own character flaws, from which we are innately protected. We are deluding ourselves. Depression knows no boundaries. From the poet Sylvia Platt to President Abraham Lincoln, depression has and will continue to afflict even those individuals whose character is beyond reproach.

The ingredients for major depression stew within the lives of every compulsive overeater. Whether or not an episode has reached its boiling point in you remains to be seen.

Depression Self Assessment

The following questionnaire will help determine if you have reached a state of major depression. Answer each of the nine symptom-oriented questions with either a YES or NO. Consider both your own personal feelings as well as what others might observe in you. To qualify as a YES, the symptom must cause you significant distress and last for at least two weeks. Don't answer YES to a question if the symptom is clearly due to a physical condition (i.e. don't mark YES to feeling fatigued if you are just getting over a bout of pneumonia).

YES   NO

____   ____   1. I am depressed most of the day,
                    nearly every day.

____   ____   2. I have lost interest or pleasure in
                    almost all of my daily life.

____   ____   3. I have had a significant (and un-
                    planned) increase/decrease in my
                    weight or my appetite.

____   ____   4. I sleep too much, or I have insomnia
                    nearly every day.

____   ____   5. I am so agitated, or conversely, so
                    sluggish that others have noticed a
                    difference in my behavior.

____   ____   6. I feel as though I have no energy.

____   ____   7. I feel worthless and/or guilty.

____   ____   8. I feel indecisive, as though I can't
                    concentrate.

____   ____   9. I wish I were dead, or I have thoughts
                    of harming myself.

Scoring

This questionnaire is based on the diagnostic criterion for major depression. If you answered YES to either question 1 or 2, and have a total of five or more affirmative responses, it is quite likely that you are suffering from major depression—of course there are a few disclaimers.

First, there can't be a physical explanation for your symptoms such as a thyroid problem, brain cancer, or a medication side effect. Second, the disturbance can't be a normal reaction to the death of a loved one. Finally, your depression can't be a part of a more serious psychiatric illness like schizophrenia.

If your score on this self assessment suggests you are depressed, help is available. Even if your score doesn't reflect depression, yet you have thoughts of harming yourself, or wish you were dead, then please see a mental health professional as soon as possible.

No this doesn't mean you're crazy, and you certainly won't end up in a padded cell. But like diabetes or hypertension, major depression is an illness that requires medical attention. Today, more than 85% of all patients with major depression can be successfully treated. It's just a simple matter of...

...Doctoring Depression

I remember going to the circus for the first time as a child and being terrified of the high wire act. As I looked up and saw some poor sap perched on a narrow cable two hundred feet above the Lion's cage, I wanted to yell, "Somebody call the police! This guy is nuts!" I mean it's not like he was carefully trying to shimmy his way across this thread of steel. Nope, he was actually riding his bicycle. To make matters worse, the doofus wasn't even holding onto the handle bars; instead, he was carrying a twenty-foot pole across his waist. I could not bare to watch this fiasco unfold.

Eventually, my mother pried my hands away from my fear-stricken eyes. To my surprise, the acrobat traversed this divide with the greatest of ease. She explained to me that this was all just part of the show and that the pole he was using was not, as I imagined, part of some ritualistic three-ring suicide. Instead, it was specially crafted to balance the performer and steady his journey to safety. Wow, pretty cool. My trip to the circus was happy again–at least until that whole clown-in-the-cannon tragedy, but that's another story altogether.

What does any of this have to do with you? Well, safely negotiating your way off the pathway to depression can be just as difficult as crossing a tight rope on your bicycle. If you have reached the point in your addiction where you are teetering to and fro on the highwire of despair, it's time to grab hold of a ballast and steady yourself. You too need a balance to carry yourself to safety. For compulsive overeaters with major depression, that balance comes from two distinct interventions: psychotherapy and medication.

Psychotherapy

Are you conjuring up images of lying back on a soft leather couch and free associating while some hardened old psychiatrist scratches his beard, mutters AH HAH, and interprets your dreams? Sorry, but you're a couple of decades too late. Talk therapy in the 1990s takes a dynamic "here and now" approach that's notably more interactive, brief, and goal-oriented. Benefits that once took years to achieve are now attainable within months.

With over two hundred different forms of psychotherapy available, choosing one that's right for you is like channel surfing with your TV's remote control. You can either sit there flipping frantically between stations, or you can relax and watch some quality programming. Because when it comes to treating major depression, there are only three therapeutic programs that demonstrate the consistent quality you deserve: *cognitive*, *behavioral*, and *interpersonal* therapy.

Cognitive Therapy: Remember Leonard Nemoy's *In Search Of?* I watched it every week and always gained some new perspective. Take England's Stonehenge for example. I used to think it was just a big pile of rocks thrown in a circle. But thanks to Leonard, I now understand that it is actually a sophisticated observatory dating back to 3000 BC. Changing perspectives is what cognitive therapy is all about.

Correcting your negative perspectives about compulsive overeating is one way to overcome major depression. Do you find yourself saying, "My overeating is all my fault?" Well throw that thought away! Replace it with a new perspective: "Through no fault of my own, I have a chemical imbalance that compels me to overeat." How about the other negative things you tell yourself like, "I'm weak and powerless?" Throw those thoughts away too. Instead, try telling yourself, "I'm strong because I've survived this illness without the understanding of others." The power to change perspectives is the power to change your life. Cognitive therapy gives you this power.

Behavioral Therapy: Behavioral therapy is like the Bob Villa's *Home Show* of psychotherapies. For example, put me in a room with six planks of wood, thirty nails, and a hammer. Come back in two hours and what will you find? ME, still sitting in a room with six planks of wood, thirty nails, and a hammer. Why? Because I'm helpless! But put Bob Villa in that room with me and two hours later I've made a barbecue pit, matching end tables, and a shoe rack! That's behavioral therapy—learning to reconstruct helplessness into action.

What sort of helplessness requires reconstruction in your life? How about the helplessness caused by an appetite that's out of control? If so, then The Menu For Life is your personal trainer. This revolutionary food plan (to be discussed) teaches you to eliminate cravings, stabilize serotonin, and maintain weight loss. Want to reverse the helplessness of major depression? Then take action. Try phoning friends when you are lonely, doing a purposeful activity when you are bored, and treating yourself to something special every now and then. In other words, add a little behavioral therapy to your life.

Interpersonal Therapy: I turned on the TV the other day and watched something called *The Montel Williams' Show*. I just didn't get it. They called it a talk show, but nobody was talking. They were ranting, raving, cursing, and even WHOOOPing, but they sure weren't talking. Luckily, a *Barbara Walter's Special* followed and restored my faith in humanity. Now this was a real talk show. Sensitive, honest, warm, and insightful–a prime time masterpiece.

That Barbara sure knows how to communicate, but most compulsive overeaters don't. That's why there's interpersonal therapy. Interpersonal therapy counteracts depression by guiding you into healthier, happier, and more open relationships. Depression clears as you learn to assert your needs, share your wants, and express your feelings without feeding them–and definitely without WHOOOPing.

Cognitive therapy adds perspective, behavioral therapy adds action, and interpersonal therapy adds expression. But which one adds serotonin? (Come on now–you know I couldn't possibly write a whole page without somehow tying in serotonin.) The answer–they all do! Imagine that. Psychotherapy changes neurochemistry. Well it does; in fact, in one recent study, just a few weeks of psychotherapy produced dramatic changes in serotonin levels. Not a bad testimony for mind over matter. But alas, sometimes the "matter" of major depression can be a high wall to hurdle. When you are severely down, psychotherapy alone may not provide all the lift you need to scale these walls. In cases like this, you just might need an extra lift. You might need...

...Antidepressants

"But Doc, I don't want medication." If I've heard that once, I've heard it a thousand times. Who in their right mind wants medication? I've never had anyone do back flips or scream, "Yippie!" when I suggested an antidepressant.

Nobody wants medication–nobody! But as Mick Jagger says, "You can't always get what you want–but sometimes, you get what you need." Some people need antidepressants! Why? Because they work!

Antidepressants have revolutionized the treatment of major depression. Clinically, they correct faulty levels of various neurotransmitters–sort of like resetting your brain's emotional thermostat. Unfortunately, resetting your emotional thermostat takes time. You can't just flick a switch like you do at home and experience instant comfort. It's more like calling the heating/air conditioning technician to come flick the switch for you, and then waiting several weeks for him/her to show up. Sometimes, antidepressants take six to eight weeks before patients experience noticeable improvement. That's the bad news. The good news is that it's worth the wait. Why? Because when properly prescribed, antidepressants completely reverse the symptoms of major depression in eight out of ten cases.

You may have noticed that I said various neurotransmitters can be faulty when it comes to major depression. You see, all roads that lead to depression do not necessarily pass through serotonin. As president of the Serotonin Fan Club, you know it breaks my heart to admit this; but sometimes, disruptions of other neurotransmitters (like norepinephrine or dopamine) play a role in the onset of mood disorders. Fortunately, antidepressants are now available that can correct each of these dysfunctioning systems.

There are three main categories of antidepressants: Tricyclic Acids (TCAs), Monoamine Oxidase Inhibitors (MAOIs), and Selective Serotonin Reuptake Inhibitors (SSRIs). Which one is the most effective? Statistically speaking (for those of you who speak Statistical) at the right dose and at the right duration, they are equally effective. All antidepressants help approximately eight out of ten patients recover from major depression. But I never learned to speak Statistical. I learned a completely different language–Practical. And practically speaking, there are substantial differences among the various antidepressants. Some, like the TCAs and MAOIs, are clearly much more complicated to use than others.

Both the TCAs (which include Pamelor, Tofranil, Sinequan, Elavil, etc.) and the MAOIs (which include Nardil, Parnate, etc.) have been available for more than forty years. If you can imagine driving around in a forty year old car, then you have some idea of the problems encountered with TCAs and MAOIs. Don't get me wrong. They will still get you to your destination. It's just that the ride can be a little rough.

You see, in addition to correcting the chemical imbalances associated with major depression, TCAs and MAOIs alter several other chemical systems that just happen to get in their way. (Picture the chemical equivalent of a speed-bump.) Here's where the ride gets rough. Most of these other chemical systems do not like being disturbed. So they demonstrate their annoyance in the form of side effects. These include dry mouth, dizziness, blurred vision, constipation, drowsiness, and *weight gain*. Additionally, MAOIs interact badly with certain foods and can potentially produce fatal elevations in blood pressure. Consequently, many patients have a tough time taking these medications for a long enough period of time to adequately treat their depression. Are they effective? Statistically speaking...yes, very! But practically speaking, how effective can a medication be if patients aren't willing to take it? Don't answer. In the language of Practical, that's a rhetorical question.

Improvements to the TCAs and MAOIs came along from time to time, but there were no major breakthroughs until 1987. That's when the first SSRI, Prozac, was introduced. Since then, two other SSRIs (Zoloft and Paxil) have received FDA approval for the treatment of major depression. SSRIs are unique because they act primarily upon serotonin. Since they don't tinker much with other chemical systems, they are tolerated far better than the older antidepressants. Although occasionally, even the SSRIs hit a "pothole" along their journey.

Side effects including nausea, diarrhea, headache, and anxiety may occur; but typically these don't last much longer than a week or two. By contrast, the side effects created by the TCAs and MAOIs often persist for months on end. So it's easy to see why the SSRIs have rapidly become the antidepressant of choice for over twenty million patients worldwide. Are SSRIs a cure-all for major depression? No. Not even close. Like other antidepressants, SSRIs have their limitations. After all, medications that effect only serotonin won't help much if your depression is caused by an imbalance of a different neurochemical. So the search for the perfect antidepressant continues. Several novel antidepressants (Wellbutrin, Serzone, Effexor, etc.) are now available, and many more are on the way. While these new drugs are promising, so far none have equaled the success of the SSRIs. This is especially true for depressed compulsive overeaters whose serotonin systems are undeniably in disarray. When major depression strikes a food addict, SSRIs are nothing short of a pharmacologic miracle. At least that's what Jane thinks.

And She Lived Happily Ever After

Jane did something that 85% of depressed Americans do not do. She got help. She saw Dr. Dixon, the hospital's psychiatrist. He surprised her from the very start. He didn't speak with a thick German accent, he had no beard to scratch, and he wasn't even wearing the horn-rimmed bifocals she envisioned. On the contrary, he appeared relatively contemporary. He smiled, was engaging, and even allowed her a moment to make herself comfortable. Dare she think it, "He seemed normal."

He began by asking Jane why she chose to see him. As Jane recounted her tale of uncontrollable bingeing, weight gain, and worsening hopelessness, Dr. Dixon did something completely unexpected. He listened! No shuffling of papers. No glancing at his watch. He didn't even interrupt her. He actually sat there and listened to what she had to say.

As the interview concluded, Dr. Dixon told Jane that she

was suffering from two illnesses: major depression and compulsive overeating. He explained that both conditions were brought on by the same treatable chemical imbalance and that overeating was her body's attempt to medicate itself. But these attempts were failing, so he offered Jane alternatives.

Over the next few months, Dr. Dixon helped Jane rediscover herself. She participated in brief psychotherapy, modified her diet, and began taking Prozac to successfully medicate her ailing serotonin system.

Did Jane *want* medication? Of course not, but she knew she *needed* it. Besides, 20 milligrams of Prozac was a whole lot easier to swallow than fifteen dollars worth of junk food. By journey's end, Jane had lost weight, gained hope, and learned to embrace life. In other words, Jane stepped off the pathway to depression and onto the road of recovery!

Chapter 6

Treating Overeating
Part I

Confessions of a Bad Mechanic

Nothing comes closer to a Sherman tank than my very first car, a 1969 Pontiac Catalina. One time I accidentally backed into a five-foot tall brick retaining wall. The wall collapsed as if blasted by the trumpets at Jericho. My car wasn't even scratched. But enough about my less than stellar driving skills. This story is about my even more atrocious mechanical skills.

I barely had the car a month when it began to utter a hideous metallic screech. I did everything a certified mechanic would do to stifle the noise. I kicked the tires, looked under the hood—heck, I even took a gander at that dipstick thingamajig. But despite such obvious mechanical genius, the lousy noise persisted. Then, EUREKA! The solution hit me. Turning up the radio really loud made the screech disappear. All Righty! Problem solved. Every time the sound resurfaced, I'd crank the volume higher—BINGO, no more screeching. Thankfully my speakers blew before my eardrums did. Only then did I discover that I had driven the last 1,500 miles with my exhaust pipe scraping along the pavement.

Why am I sharing this poignant tale of my idiocy? Because my quick fix approach to car care is like the food addict's folly with dieting. It treated the symptoms but ignored the cause.

The "give it a week and we'll take off the weight" philosophy might help the average person lose weight, but it doesn't work for compulsive overeaters. All you are doing is treating a symptom of the disease while disregarding the addiction. Until you eliminate the foods that rain chaos on your serotonin system, the biology of compulsive overeating will never be managed.

Just Say NO!

Preach that the alcoholic abstain from alcohol, and the choir shouts, "Hallelujah." Preach that the crack addict give up cocaine, and the congregation rejoices. But preach that the compulsive overeater eliminate binge food, and the flock becomes angered. "BLASPHEMY!" they scoff and cry, "Why must our brothers and sisters resist the temptation of sugary sweet goodness?" It's simple. You have to or it will destroy you. *Thou shalt abstain from binge food* must be the food addict's eleventh commandment.

Abstinence is nothing more than avoiding harmful chemicals that habitually alter your behavior, mood, and brain. It is an essential principle in the recovery from any addiction. Food addiction is no exception. For compulsive overeaters, abstinence means avoiding foods that pacify emotion and manipulate serotonin.

Abstinence rids your body of the "confectious" toxins

that chemically bind feeding with feelings. With abstinence, the cycle of addiction can finally be broken. Once free from binge food's ruinous grasp, the mad-mad ride on the serotonin roller coaster can finally come to an end. There will be no more tryptophan powered serotonin spikes and no more negative feedback loops to plunge serotonin levels into the ground. Instead, your body's internal factory can get back on line, producing serotonin in a controlled, even manner. Food will no longer rule your thoughts and deeds. You will!

For many, the biologic treatment of compulsive overeating begins and ends with this simple commitment to abstinence. Simple, that is, once you accept abstinence as a commitment for life. That's right–life! Abstinence is not a diet. You don't "go on" abstinence for a week to look better in your bikini. Just as the alcoholic must permanently swear off alcohol or risk relapse, so too must the compulsive overeater abstain from his/her binge food–forever!

Cheer up. Don't mourn the loss of binge food from your life. Remember, a wise sage once said, "Abstinence makes the heart grow fonder." All right, so I took some poetic liberties with that quotation, but the principle still applies. Abstinence is not about loss. It's about growth. Author, therapist, and former compulsive overeater, Anne Katherine, embraces this positive outlook on abstinence. She believes abstinence offers the recovering food addict five wonderful blessings: emotional stability, freedom from food cravings, vibrant participation in life, and increased awareness of yourself as a distinct, unique, and worthy human being. I couldn't agree more. Once you say good-bye to binge food, you say hello to life.

A Little Help from My Friends

You would think after dragging my muffler 1,500 miles through the potholes of Pittsburgh that I wouldn't have much of a muffler left. But like I said, that Pontiac was a tank. Aside from a few dents and dings, the exhaust system was still exhausting, the muffler was still muffling—well you get the picture. Everything worked.

I know sharing this next part of the story won't exactly place me in the Mechanic's Hall of Fame, but that's life. Anyway, there I was, under the belly of this beastly Pontiac, bubbling with testosterone. I, Mr. Goodwrench, had finally figured out the cause of the screeching. I was proud. I was strong. I was manly. I was clueless.

Yep, clueless! Even though I knew what was wrong, I had no idea how to fix it. Fortunately, I had friends who did. Friends who said, "You need to buy this type of clamp." "Here, brace this pipe against the chassis." "HEY! Don't touch the exhaust. It's still hot!" (Ouch! They told me that a few seconds too late.)

Anyhow, with the support and guidance of a few friends, I successfully treated both the cause and effect of my problem. Once again, I was back on the highway motoring along my merry way—this time, in silence.

When traveling along the highways of abstinence, you too may need a few friends to guide and support you. Hopefully, one of your best friends will be The Menu For Life. This serotonin-friendly meal plan makes everyday abstinence a simple reality. It's your very own "tutor" for nutritionally managing compulsive overeating, without needless obsession. But as tempting as it may be to dive right into The Menu For Life, read on. Sadly for some, just saying NO to binge food still isn't enough to battle the biology of compulsive overeating.

Dear Abby

Abigail missed our last eight group sessions. But as fate would have it, we literally bumped into each other while rounding a corner at the local mall. To my surprise, Abby turned away and made a shame-ridden dash toward the exit. I quickly called out, "Abby, the group really misses you." With that, she stopped dead in her tracks and sobbed,

"Why should they miss me? I'm a failure. Nothing works. I just bring the whole group down."

Abby regained her composure and began explaining that even though she was following The Menu For Life to the letter, she still craved sweets, continued to cry at the drop of a hat, and hadn't lost any weight. "Don't get me wrong," she said, "I'm not bingeing anymore, and I don't let food govern my thoughts. But quite frankly, my life just isn't transformed like the rest of the group's. Face it Doc, I'm hopeless."

Abby wasn't hopeless. But what was stopping her from making the progress she deserved? Was it Abby? Was she somehow sabotaging The Menu For Life? Not likely. Abby is one of the brightest accountants I know. Her attention to detail is flawless. When Abby said that she followed The Menu For Life to the letter, I didn't doubt her. Then was it The Menu For Life that failed? Again, not likely. Abstinence has helped thousands overcome compulsive overeating. So if it wasn't Abby and it wasn't The Menu For Life, what was the trouble? That's right. Trouble! Right here in River City. With a capitol T, and that rhymes with G, and that stands for—Genetics.

Gene Therapy

Abby's husband, Gene, learned about his high blood pressure during his last physical exam. Since then, he exercised daily, lost weight, and greatly reduced the amount of salt in his diet. In short, Gene made all the necessary behavioral changes to lower his blood pressure. Was he successful? Not exactly. In fact, when he returned for his next check up, his blood pressure was even higher.

Naturally Gene was disappointed, but unlike Abby, he didn't consider himself a failure. He knew that hypertension was genetic, and sometimes, all the good clean living in the world won't win the war against heredity.

The same holds true for compulsive overeaters. Sometimes, despite the right behavioral interventions, the brain's serotonin system can remain dysfunctional. On these occasions, counseling, stress management, relaxation, and even The Menu For Life can't halt the addictive cycle.

Abby wasn't failing and neither was Gene–their chromosomes were. There was no self-help strategy that was strong enough to conquer their diseases. Both needed an even stronger weapon. They needed medication. For Gene, the choices seemed limitless. There were dozens of antihypertensive medications to choose from. But what about the Abbys of the world? Can they be helped? Is there a medicine that can control compulsive overeating?

Waist (Waste) Products

Each year consumers pay thirty-three billion hard earned dollars to control their appetites and lose weight. With that much cash at stake, you can bet that everyone, from the well-meaning expert to the low-down dirty hustler, will be trying to grab their share of the wealth; and there's no easier way to milk this weight loss cash cow then to offer Americans what Americans like best–the quick fix–the Minute Rice of medication–the diet pill. No need to waste time with such trivial concerns as watching what you eat, managing stress, or exercise. Nah! Just take these pills and call my answering service in the morning.

Maybe I wouldn't be so sarcastic if these "magic beans" offered compulsive overeaters even a glimmer of hope. Unfortunately, they do not. That's certainly the case with the prototypical "doctor prescribed" appetite suppressants like Ionamin, Fastin, Adipex, and Phentermine. These drugs are nothing more than toned down versions of amphetamine, or "speed." They crank up the volume on your entire body but do zilch to quiet your screeching serotonin system. Not only do they have the potential to cause strokes and heart attacks, they are also potentially addictive. The last thing any compulsive overeater needs is another addiction.

Then there is Fenfluramine (Redux or Pondimin), the newest prescription to stand center circle in today's diet drug circus. It increases serotonin function, reduces the urge to binge, and promotes significant weight loss. Seems perfect, right? Oh yeah, one more thing—one of the primary side effects of fenfluramine is depression. You're at risk for that as it is. Do you really want to tempt fate? What's worse, research suggests that fenfluramine is chemically related to the designer drug *Ecstasy*. Over the long run, it may actually destroy serotonin—and if that's not scary enough, then take a look at this.

Remember the simple rules of childhood—share, eat your vegetables, and two wrongs don't make a right. I learned them. You learned them. Everybody learned them. Unfortunately, somewhere along the line, the diet industry tried to change the "two wrongs don't make a right" rule.

The latest fad is to combine phentermine (an amphetamine derivative that is potentially addictive) with fenfluramine (the drug that can lead to depression and destroy serotonin). It just doesn't make sense. Yes, this "phen/fen" combo creates a significant degree of weight loss; but let's face it, so do tapeworms and food poisoning. Anyone care for a concoction of rotten eggs and leeches? I didn't think so. So why are more and more overweight Americans turning to this volatile mixture of phentermine and fenfluramine? It's for the same reasons they are willing to subject themselves to stomach staplings and jaw wirings: false hope and frantic desperation to find the ultimate quick fix.

The trouble is, nobody (*not even your doctor*) knows the long-term side effects of these two drugs. In fact, within the last few months, several individuals taking this "miracle fix" have developed a rare and fatal heart/lung disease. Because of this, the manufacturers of Redux/fenfluramine have voluntarily removed these products from the market. So, I guess that the rule hasn't changed after all. Two wrongs still don't make a right. They make an even bigger wrong!

What about nonprescription appetite suppressants?

Well, they aren't addictive, and they don't seem to cause depression, but they sure aren't anything to "sneeze" at. Why? Because the most popular brands, like Dexatrim, contain the active ingredient, *phenylpropanolamine.* What wonder of modern medicine is phenylpropanolamine? It's the same wonder that helps stop sniffles and clear stuffy heads in Dimetapp, Triaminic, Alka Seltzer Plus, and Halls Mentho-Lyptus. Yep! It's cold medicine. Appetite suppression is just one of its many side effects. It may help those who "starve a cold and feed a fever," but it's no treatment for compulsive overeating.

As for the rest of the pills and potions that promise to melt fat or burn calories, about the only thing getting burned and melted will be the inside of your wallet. These "natural diet aides" invariably contain caffeine, laxative, ephedra, or just plain snake oil—none are effective for the long-term management of obesity. None! Money spent on this nonsense truly puts the "waste" in waist reduction.

Building a Better Mouse Trap

You don't have to be Nostradamus to predict the futility of conventional diet pills. Quick fixes are never the answers to lifelong problems. Compulsive overeating is a chronic condition that requires chronic treatment. Fortunately, scientists are beginning to recognize the shortcomings of today's appetite suppressants. New guidelines have been formulated to help foster more enduring medical interventions for compulsive overeating. According to psychopharmacologist, Dr. Michelle Towle:

If anti-bingeing/obesity drugs are to be used successfully for the long-term, they must have the following properties:

1. The medication must significantly reduce the desire to binge.
2. The medication must have a weight-lowering effect that is clinically proven and sustained.

3. The medication must be well tolerated with few side effects and no long-term health hazards.
4. The medication must not be addictive.

Over the past few years, there has been an explosion of research on one particular medication that appears to possess all of these properties. So what is this wonder drug, you ask? Believe it or not, it is **Prozac**. Yes, Prozac! The miraculous, yet controversial pill that has reclaimed the lives of the sad, the anxious, and the irritable, now stands poised to challenge the most refractory of disorders: Food Addiction!

Prozac may be of particular benefit to compulsive overeaters because it works by enhancing the body's serotonin system. Technically, Prozac delays the brain's metabolism of serotonin, making more available for the brain's neurochemical soup. Drawing on our original analogy, this delay allows the "message in a bottle" (serotonin) to remain at sea longer and improve communication with the surrounding neurons.

Looking at it another way, Prozac gives the food addict a superior alternative to bingeing. Sugar and highly processed carbohydrates supply only a temporary and erratic boost in serotonin; but Prozac provides a sustained, consistent, and above all, calorie-free way to optimize the compulsive overeater's serotonin system.

All this sounds great in theory. But who wants theory? We want results! Unfortunately, getting these results is going to take some good old-fashioned scientific research. OOOH! Sounds boring. Well, thank goodness someone did it for us. Let's look at what they found.

Rats! Not Again?

Oh yes, rats! Lots of them. When it comes to research, there is no greater vermin martyr than the lab rat. Scientists have rats for just about every occasion. Need a rat with diabetes? They have it. How about one with cancer? They have that too. So if you are studying Prozac and obesity, you will need a fat rat. No problem. Meet the Zucker rat. Zucker rats are a special breed of rat guaranteed to be obese. All the Zucker girls and boys, aunts and uncles, nieces and nephews, and so on, are genetically engineered to be downright huge. Scientists took these Zuckers, fed them their own special blend of Prozac Rat Chow, and then sat back and watched what happened.

The results hardly came as a surprise. When obese rats were given Prozac to increase their serotonin levels, they ate less, ate more slowly, and felt full faster. Not only did the Zucker rats lose weight, they were able to maintain their weight loss as long as the Prozac was given. That differs dramatically from the effect amphetamine-like diet pills have on Zuckers. If you give a Zucker some amphetamine, it will initially lose weight; but after a while, the drug seems to lose its power and the rat again becomes heavy. This phenomenon is known as tolerance and it doesn't seem to occur in the Prozac treated rats.

Another remarkable difference emerged between the Zuckers treated with Prozac and those treated with conventional diet pills. Even though the Prozac treated rats nibbled on less calories, the amount of protein they ate remained about the same. In other words, the Prozac-Zuckers lost weight by choosing to eat fewer carbohydrates and fat. On the other hand, the amphetamine-Zuckers lost their appetite for all food, including protein. This distinction is very important to compulsive overeaters because protein is required to maintain muscle mass. If you lose your appetite for protein, you risk losing muscle instead of fat. More importantly, these studies suggest that Prozac can selectively limit the consumption of the very substances that trigger food addiction: highly processed carbohydrates, sugar, and excess fat.

As impressive as these results may seem, researchers still weren't satisfied. After all, scientists just can't have fun with lab rats until they have completely tormented the poor rodents in the name of progress. And so they did. Believe it or not, Zucker rats (like food addicts) overeat when they feel stressed. So how do you stress a rat? Personally, I would wallpaper its cage with pictures of cats, but that's not how the researchers went about it. Instead, they discovered that repeatedly pinching a Zucker's tail caused it to become pretty darn uptight. And when a Zucker is uptight, a Zucker is hungry. Real hungry! Standard diet pills have never quenched the hunger of a tail pinched, tense Zucker. They'd just keep gnawing away. But Prozac proved to be different. Zuckers treated with Prozac can cope with this stress and no longer binge.

All this may come as good news to the Zucker clan, but let's face it, rats and people just don't have much in common. For one thing, pinching a rat's tail is considered a stress test. But try that on a person, and all of a sudden it's sexual harassment! The point is, animal studies can provide only so much insight into human behavior. The true test of Prozac's ability to control compulsive overeating can only come from human studies.

Final Exams

Double Blind? I know that probably sounds like a Nintendo game, but actually it's the way scientists study medications. Here's how it works. Participants are first divided into random halves. One-half receives the active drug (in our case, Prozac), and the other half receives a *placebo*, a pill that looks just like the active drug, but really doesn't contain anything. Neither the researchers nor the volunteers know exactly who is taking what until the study is complete and the results are ready to be tabulated.

This probably seems like overkill. After all, what can a placebo filled with nothing possibly do to someone? Well, the answer is plenty. The "placebo effect" can be powerful. In most cases, approximately 40% of people given "nothing" will still report "something," either good or bad. Some feel dizzy, nauseous, or tired, while others describe insomnia or agitation. Still others report a complete resolution of the very symptoms the active pill was designed to treat. By comparing the placebo to the active drug, researchers can sort out those effects that are genuinely attributable to the medication versus those that are more mind over matter. Inspired by willingness and quiet desperation, thousands of overweight Americans have given their hope, time, and bodies to participate in Prozac double blind anti-obesity studies. Researchers from across the nation have picked, poked, and prodded these volunteers in order to fully test the weight-lowering/anti-bingeing potential of this amazing medication. Testing varied from site to site, but all offered answers to the same central questions: Does Prozac possess the qualities required of a safe, effective, long-term anti-compulsive overeating drug? Can it help the "Abbys" among us? Does it have the right stuff to pass our final exam?

Our final exam will be to break down Dr. Towle's guidelines point by point and see how Prozac compares. So without further delay, let's review the Prozac Report Card.

REQUIREMENT 1

The medication must significantly reduce the desire to binge.

EVALUATION

Several published studies, including one in the prestigious *Journal of Clinical Psychiatry,* conclude that Prozac causes a substantial and sustained reduction in bingeing. But I think Janelle, one of my most candid clients, summed up Prozac's anti-bingeing properties best by stating, "I can finally apply the brakes to my appetite without skidding out of control."

So how does Prozac reduce bingeing when so many other drugs have tried and failed? It's simple. Prozac is the first of a new generation of medicines (SSRIs) that mimics the effects of binge food and fools your body into thinking it's full. Both Prozac and binge food increase serotonin in the "feeding" and "feeling" parts of the brain. HPCs, sugar, and excess fat accomplish this only briefly and also carry the burden of additional calories. Prozac, however, achieves more enduring results without unwanted calories. As a result, volunteers treated with Prozac react like Zuckers. They eat fewer carbohydrate snacks, less total calories, and feel full faster. In other words, *Prozac significantly reduces the desire to binge.* With this kind of success, it's no wonder Prozac is the only medication to receive FDA approval for the treatment of bulimia.

REQUIREMENT 2

The medication must have a weight-lowering effect that is clinically proven and sustained.

EVALUATION

Since 1987, over three dozen double blind/placebo control studies have demonstrated Prozac's superior ability to promote weight loss. The earliest studies lasted only eight weeks. But even in this short time frame, obese volunteers given a daily dose of Prozac and no specific diet or exercise instruction lost an average of ten pounds compared to only four pounds lost by those receiving placebo. A six pound difference may not seem like a big deal, but it represents a 150% improvement over the placebo.

Long-term studies have met with similar success. More than 3,500 overweight participants can attest to this. In a recently completed 52 week Prozac/placebo trial, individuals receiving Prozac lost as much as five times the weight as those taking placebo. In fact, the average weekly weight loss of volunteers taking Prozac, at an anti-obesity/purging dose, exceeds that of all current appetite suppressants, including Redux.

But needless to say, Prozac doesn't promote endless weight loss. As time passes, like all anti-obesity medications, Prozac's effect plateaus. In the above studies, most volunteers continued to lose weight for upwards of seven months, after which little additional weight loss occurred. Does this mean that Prozac stopped working? Not at all. Prozac continued to help patients maintain their weight loss. You see, some of the volunteers discontinued Prozac at the end of the initial study. To no one's surprise, they started gaining weight. Six months later, the volunteers who stopped Prozac regained about one-third of their lost weight.

So what became of the volunteers that remained on Prozac? Most ended up weighing significantly less than when they started. More importantly, within this population of weight loss achievers, two groups lost more weight than all the rest—approximately 14% of their total body weight. "Which two," you ask? The two that combined either behavior modification or nutrition counseling with their Prozac treatment. Aah, Lucky you! The rest of *Chocolate is My Kryptonite* is all about behavior and nutrition. Wow, what a bargain.

But alas, all is not wine and roses. Some volunteers experienced very little change in weight. Is this cause for concern? Not really. Unfortunately, these studies included patients with all forms of obesity, not just compulsive overeating. It's my guess that patients who didn't respond to Prozac were overweight for reasons other than binge eating. Perhaps they didn't need the adjustment in serotonin that Prozac provides—the adjustment that some compulsive overeaters absolutely require—the adjustment that took Abby from a size 16 to a size 10—the adjustment that led study after study to the same conclusion: Prozac promotes weight loss.

REQUIREMENT 3

The medication must be well tolerated with few side effects and no long-term health hazards.

EVALUATION

The largest Prozac/anti-obesity study to date concluded: "Prozac is effective, well tolerated, and safe in the treatment

of obesity." This doesn't mean that Prozac is completely free
of side effects. It is a powerful medication that some people
can't tolerate. Nevertheless, Prozac has an exceptionally low
rate of side effects (most of which are mild, infrequent, and
short-lived). They include:

Headache	20%	*Diarrhea*	12%
Nausea	20%	*Anxiety*	11%
Insomnia	14%	*Sweating*	8%
Fatigue	12%	*Tremor*	8%

These complaints were typically voiced during the first
two weeks of treatment, after which they generally sub-
sided. Very few patients chose to discontinue their medication due to any bothersome effects. In fact, nearly all were
willing to put up with these inconveniences in order to finally manage their disease.

What are some of the least common side effects of Prozac?
Well, if you looked up aspirin in any medical textbook, you
would find a frightening list of side effects including: hear-
ing loss, bleeding, and polyps. Before long, the list itself
would scare the fever right out of you. The point is, every
drug in existence reports a virtually endless list of adverse
reactions. Most are as rare as hen's teeth, but listing them
protects both the patient and the manufacturer. Prozac is no
exception. Several hundred potential side effects ranging
from excessive yawning to convulsion have been reported.
Thankfully, most of these complaints occur in far fewer than
1% of patients. Nevertheless, it is important not to discount
any ill-effects without notifying your physician. A complete
list of Prozac's side effects can be obtained at your local li-
brary. Just ask for the *Physicians' Desk Reference*®.

Finally, there are no known or foreseeable dangers associated with the long-term use of Prozac. But keep in mind,
Prozac has been available only since 1987. Experts believe
that drugs need to be tested for twenty-five years before all
conceivable risks are assessed. So until the year 2012, the
question of long-term health hazards will remain unanswered. Most compulsive overeaters aren't willing to wait!

REQUIREMENT 4

The medication must not be addictive.

EVALUATION

For a chemical to be addictive, there must be a state of dependence that leads to social, emotional, or physical harm. In the past decade, twenty million patients were placed on Prozac–and guess what? Not one has knocked over a Revco to get an extra fix, and nobody has been spotted lurking around darkened street corners trying to score a capsule or two. In short, there is no evidence that suggests Prozac is in any way habit forming or addictive. Patients who are doing well on Prozac do not need a higher and higher dose to maintain the same results. Likewise, there are no withdrawal symptoms when patients discontinue use.

And the Winner is???

No need to grade on a curve, Prozac definitely passes our final exam. Heck, compared to traditional diet pills, Prozac deserves to be valedictorian. But does this mean that every compulsive overeater should take Prozac? No! No! And one more time with volume...**NO!**

This isn't a book about pills, potions, or cure-alls. This is a book about feeding better and feeling better—for life. "Thou shalt abstain" remains the sole remedy for most compulsive overeaters. Prozac shouldn't even be considered unless your overeating has progressed to bulimia or major depression. Instead, give The Menu For Life a chance to stabilize your system. It's the only biological treatment needed for the majority of compulsive overeaters. However, if after one or two months of abstinence you are still bingeing, purging, or moody, then consider Prozac to supplement (not replace) The Menu For Life.

All right, so Prozac isn't for everyone, and it's a far cry

from a magic cure; but for our clients who need medication, Prozac is nothing short of a miracle. Donna says, "For the first time in years I'm not preoccupied with food." Jack tells me, "I can't believe the binges are gone," and Lara is pleased to say, "The dark clouds have vanished. I can finally see the light." Donna, Jack, and Lara were once considered too difficult to treat. Prozac helped change that. It offers promise for even the most treatment resistant cases of compulsive overeating—even for Abby.

Abby was thrilled to learn there was hope. She paid close attention as I summarized her situation. She even went home and phoned a few members of our support group who were taking Prozac. But Abby didn't rush her decision to start medication. She had plenty of questions. And you probably do too. So for the interested, the inquisitive, and the just plain curious, let's take a moment or two for some...

...Prozac Q&A

What are the indications for taking Prozac?

Prozac represents the first drug in an entirely new class of medication called the Selective Serotonin Reuptake Inhibitors (SSRIs). *Newsweek* called it "a breakthrough drug for depression." Although Prozac is classified as an antidepressant, physicians are using Prozac to successfully manage a variety of ailments including: panic disorder, obsessive-compulsive disorder, premenstrual syndrome, and compulsive overeating. In fact, all disorders in which serotonin dysfunction plays a major role will likely respond to Prozac.

Are there other drugs available that are similar to Prozac?

In the United States there are currently three other SSRIs available: Zoloft, Luvox, and Paxil. You may have heard of them by their respective generic names: Sertraline, Fluvoxamine, and Paroxetine. Several other SSRIs should be approved by the turn of the century. However, thus far, only Prozac has the FDA seal of approval for the treatment of bulimia.

What is the average daily dose of Prozac?

Medications must be tailored to a person's specific needs. However, on average, eating disorders are best treated with a Prozac dose that is three times larger than the standard starting dose. In healthy adults, the recommended starting dose for Prozac is 20 milligrams per day. Typically, clients are placed on this dose and monitored for side effects. Over the next few weeks, Prozac is gradually increased to its optimal dose, approximately 60 milligrams.

How much does Prozac cost?

Plenty! Without a prescription plan, the cost can be prohibitive. A one month supply of Prozac, at the above dose, is likely to cost between $100 and $175. Unfortunately, a less expensive generic version is not yet available.

Who can prescribe Prozac?

Any physician can write a prescription for Prozac, but it's best to see a doctor familiar with both eating disorders and psychopharmacology. Clients deserve to be monitored closely by someone who understands compulsive overeating and knows when to increase, decrease, or discontinue the medication.

What time of day should Prozac be taken?

Unlike many traditional diet pills, Prozac needs to be taken only once a day. Patients being treated primarily for depression or anxiety are often instructed to take their Prozac in the morning. This minimizes the likelihood of insomnia as a side effect. However, for many compulsive overeaters the effect is just the opposite. Prozac improves their sleep, so they end up taking it at bedtime. (Please consult your doctor before making any changes in your medication!)

How quickly will Prozac help?
That depends. Some benefits, such as fewer cravings and weight reduction, are noticeable within the first few days. Others, including improved mood and decreased irritability, may take longer to develop. Therefore, compulsive overeaters should not expect to see the complete range of benefits until they are on a full therapeutic dose of Prozac for at least six weeks.

Is it possible to gain weight on Prozac?
Yes, but that seldom becomes problematic for compulsive overeaters. You see, Prozac is a potent antianxiety medication. Some patients are so overwhelmed by anxiety that they are physically unable to eat. Once Prozac treats this anxiety, their appetites return and they gain weight. Compulsive overeaters, however, don't lose their appetite when anxious. Instead, their hunger increases and they binge. So as Prozac reduces both anxiety and the drive to binge, weight loss is the result.

Can you overdose on Prozac?
Not easily. You are more likely to be struck by lightening than die from a Prozac overdose. Someone even took thirty-seven times the maximum recommended dosage without suffering permanent injury. Death is indeed a rare exception. Those few who have died after taking too much Prozac invariably combined the overdose with other, more lethal, medications. In fact, most medications, including Tylenol, are far deadlier in overdose than Prozac.

I'm a compulsive overeater with diabetes. Can I take Prozac?
Absolutely. There is mounting evidence that Prozac may actually benefit obese diabetics. Several studies have demonstrated that Prozac can actually improve control of diabetics' blood sugar levels. Furthermore, this improvement is independent of Prozac's weight-lowering effect. In one study, test subjects were able to reduce their insulin requirements

by forty-four percent. Because of this, any diabetic placed on Prozac should have their blood sugar monitored, and their insulin level adjusted as needed.

What effects does Prozac have on the heart?

Not many. Even those of us with the achiest-breakiest of hearts can tolerate Prozac. Typically, it doesn't effect EKG, heart rate, or blood pressure in any significant way. Every now and then there's a report of someone having a heart attack or a funky arrhythmia shortly after starting Prozac, but these cases are extremely rare and probably just coincidental. Given a choice between the literal "heartbreak" that amphetamine-like diet pills cause, or Prozac–I'd choose Prozac in a heartbeat.

Is it safe to take Prozac with other medications?

Monoamine Oxidase Inhibitors (a powerful class of antidepressant) are the only medications that are absolutely contraindicated in patients on Prozac. Serious and sometimes fatal reactions occur when the two are combined. Aside from this, Prozac can be given in conjunction with all other medications. Drug interactions may still occur, especially if a patient is on several medications. In most cases, however, these interactions are safely and easily managed.

Can Prozac be taken during pregnancy?

Prozac is not known to cause birth defects. Animal studies using doses ten times larger than recommended, as well as anecdotal human case reports, have found no evidence that Prozac causes any fetal harm. Nevertheless, it is wise to *avoid* Prozac while trying to conceive, or to discontinue it if already pregnant. After all, most pregnancies are a little more personal than an anecdotal case report.

Likewise, Prozac is excreted into a mother's breast milk. It isn't clear what effects, if any, this might have on a infant. Knowing that it's better to be safe than sorry, postpartum patients who require Prozac probably should not nurse.

Are there other conditions where Prozac should not be prescribed?

Not really. Of course the textbooks add, "People with a known allergy to Prozac should not take it." (Gee, thanks for sharing the obvious.) But essentially, the above conditions are the only ones in which Prozac should be avoided at all costs. Of course there are other medical conditions where Prozac needs to be used cautiously.

For example, Prozac is broken down by the liver and excreted by the kidneys. So if one of these organs is ailing, then even normal doses can be toxic. "Baby doses," however, should work just fine. Caution also needs to be a priority with manic-depressive patients. Any antidepressant, including Prozac, can push this type of patient into a full-blown manic state.

The list goes on. Naturally there are illnesses in which any medication, even aspirin, should be used with discretion. Prozac is no exception. So now that I've scared the bejeebers out of you, let's set the record straight. In general, Prozac is a very safe and effective medication. Although if you have any concerns, don't hesitate to ask your doctor.

Will Prozac turn me into an axe-wielding, suicidal maniac?

Not a chance. Accusations like this may stir controversy on afternoon talk shows, but not in the medical community. Both the FDA Advisory Committee and an independent scientific panel unanimously agreed that Prozac does not cause suicidal or violent behavior. So why the negative press? Perhaps since Prozac is the best selling antidepressant ever, people expect the impossible—guaranteed prevention of suicide. But two simple truths preclude this: antidepressants don't work overnight, and depressed people often consider suicide. In fact, 15% of people with major depression eventually do kill themselves. If anything, Prozac is considered to lower their overall risk of self harm, but it can't thwart every suicidal act.

But what if you aren't depressed? What if you are on

Prozac for another condition, like compulsive overeating? Are you then at an increased risk for suicidal thoughts? Absolutely not. An analysis of over 2,000 volunteers (treated with Prozac specifically for weight loss) found absolutely no evidence that Prozac induced suicidality.

Wait one more second! What about the "Prozac defense?" Haven't lawyers argued that Prozac caused their clients to perform heinous acts of murder, violence, and assorted naughtiness? Well sure, lawyers claimed this, but they will claim just about anything to win their case. However, in more than 50 court cases brought to trial alleging Prozac caused either suicidal or violent behavior, all were either dismissed or Prozac was exonerated. In fact, many psychiatrists, including myself, successfully use Prozac to treat patients whose presenting complaint is irritability and aggression.

How long should I take Prozac when treating overeating?

Great question. Now if only I had a great answer. Trouble is, nobody knows for sure. There just isn't any data. The best we can do is make an educated guess. Unfortunately, *guess* is the operative word.

We know that compulsive overeating is a chronic disease. We also know that Prozac helps maintain weight loss even after the "reducing effect" plateaus. But more importantly, we realize that managing compulsive overeating involves a lifetime of better *feeding* and better *feeling*, and not necessarily a lifetime of medication.

I ask clients to stay on Prozac for at least six-to-nine months. While the medication is busy doing its job, my clients are busy improving their self-esteem, learning how to deal with stress, and living well on The Menu For Life. When it's finally time to stop Prozac, they've slimmed outwardly, grown inwardly, and built an entire armory of physical and emotional weapons to battle compulsive overeating.

If after Prozac is discontinued, symptoms of depression, purging, or unmerciful binges reoccur, I usually have clients restart their Prozac and consider extended treatment.

Abby's Revival

Abby took a few days to ponder these issues before deciding to augment The Menu For Life with Prozac. She began taking 20 milligrams per day. Over the next two weeks, I gradually raised her dose to 60 milligrams daily. Not long after, Abby phoned me to say, "I can't believe it. My body isn't begging for sweets anymore. I even walked by the bakery this morning without craving one of their gooey cinnamon buns."

Three weeks later, Abby returned to my office wearing something new—a smile! What a turn around. Before starting Prozac, Abby was so tight-lipped, I wasn't even sure she had teeth; and now she was looking like a walking commercial for Colgate. Of course she had every right to be grinning. After all, her sadness lifted, her cravings vanished, and she lost eight pounds. All in all, she was having a pretty darn smile-worthy month.

It is well over a year since Abby and I had our fateful collision, and she's still smiling. Abby has lost 55 pounds and has maintained her goal weight for over six months. She loves The Menu For Life and her emotional freedom; but best of all, she loves herself. Three CHEERS for Abby!

Graduation Day

Serotonin...Tryptophan...Food Addiction. Go ahead, admit it! Your brain is just about full. Whether you wanted to be or not, you are now an expert on the biology of compulsive overeating. Congratulations! Your diploma is in the mail.

Wouldn't it be great if this was the whole story, and the answer to your life long struggle was as simple as The Menu For Life and maybe, just maybe, Prozac? Unfortunately, the good things in life are not so simple. One key force still lies behind the door to recovery. Without it, compulsive overeating is destined to endure.

So just what is this missing force? I can sum it up in one word—*feelings*. That's right, feelings. Those every day emotions that each of us possess. Now you're probably asking yourself, "Since everybody has feelings, why is my appetite so out of control and my neighbor's isn't?" That's simple. Somewhere along the line you learned to deal with your own feelings by eating, overeating, and then eating some more. If you aren't sure when, where, how, or even if this happened to you–don't worry, you will. Because so far we've only explored the biology of food addiction. Now it's time to take a closer look at the psychology of compulsive overeating.

Chapter 7

Feeding Your Feelings: The Psychology of Compulsive Overeating

Food for Thought

Allow me to read your mind. Close your eyes and recall your very first food memory. It doesn't matter how old you were or how clear the memory is, just relax, and think of food and your childhood. Okay, got it? Now witness my amazing psychic powers. I bet that your first food memory falls into one of two emotional categories: *Love* or *Control*.

How did I do? Are you impressed? Are you ready to call my 1-900 psychic hotline? Well don't because it's just a trick. You see, almost all compulsive overeaters' first food memories are about love or control.

Food can seem like an amazing source of love. For example, maybe your first food memory is the smell of fresh chocolate chip cookies wafting through the air at Grandma's house. Somehow the scent made you feel safe and nurtured. Even today, the aroma of freshly baked cookies may warm your heart. Or maybe it was your birthday, the one day each year when people gathered just to celebrate you and share your cake. During these times you felt loved and special.

Now in an ideal world, you would feel loved and special all the time. Yet for many "future" compulsive overeaters, feeling loved was a very rare occurrence, but food was always there to fill the void. It gave you the loving feeling you so desperately needed.

Food can also be a source of control. Remember sitting at the dining room table for hours because you refused to eat something? My guess is that the situation was never about the spinach or the peas. It was a power struggle between a parent and a child. Your yearnings to take charge of life got mixed-up with brussel sprouts and string beans. Controlling food meant controlling life, and that felt good!

I also have many clients who grew up poor and couldn't always afford to eat what they wanted. They learned to associate eating, whenever or whatever, with being powerful. It was their way of overcoming an impoverished childhood and staking claim to the world. It made them think, "I've made it. I can eat anything I want. I'm in control!"

So what about your first food memory? Is it about love, control, or maybe both? I suppose it doesn't really matter, because some how, no matter what your first food memory is, you learned to associate feeding with feelings. Good feelings. Positive feelings. Feelings that washed away your troubles in an ocean of sugar. Feelings that made you feel better. Why? Well, that's just the nature of compulsive overeating—or maybe I should say, the **nurture** of compulsive overeating.

The nurture of compulsive overeating begins early in life with a process called conditioning. When psychologists refer to conditioning, they aren't talking about jumping jacks, free weights, or step aerobics. Instead, they are referring to a specific way of learning. In **classical conditioning**, learning occurs when a neutral event is repeatedly paired with a stimulating event that always evokes a certain response. Eventually the neutral event becomes associated with, and can independently evoke, that same response. Huh? Say what?? All right, so it's a little confusing but bare with me. It will make sense. Believe it or not, the earliest studies of conditioning involved food.

Pavlov's Dog

Nobel prize winner Ivan Pavlov had a dog. I could have spent time researching whether or not this dog was male or female, shepherd or spaniel, neutered or frisky, but I didn't. Let's just assume it was your plain old run-of-the-mill four-pawed, wet nosed, tail wagging dog. We'll be extra original and call it Spot. Like any normal dog, Spot started drooling whenever Pavlov brought out its bowl full of Alpo.

Maybe Pavlov was an aristocrat, because whenever he brought Spot's dinner, he would also ring a bell. (Ring! Ring! Dinner is served.) Spot would then see the Alpo and start drooling. Everyday the cycle would repeat: Bell-Food-Drool, Bell-Food-Drool, Bell-Food-Drool.

I'm guessing that one day Pavlov went to get Spot's supper and, to steal a line from Mother Goose, "All the cupboards were bare." Perhaps out of habit, he rang the dinner bell anyway. Well what do you know, even though there was no food in sight, Spot commenced to slobber, salivate, and drool just as if Alpo was raining from heaven.

Go ahead, ring a bell in front of your own dog and see what happens. Maybe its ears will crop up or its head will tilt the way it does when you confuse it, but I'll bet that you won't have a puddle of dog spit at your feet—unless of course you have a Saint Bernard, and then it's just a part of life.

So what was the deal with Pavlov's dog? Conditioned learning. Spot was conditioned to associate the bell (neutral event) with food (stimulating event), which always resulted in slobber (evoked response). In time, the bell conditioned the slobber response all by itself. Behavioral psychologists call the bell a **conditioned event**, food an **unconditioned event**, and drooling to a bell a **conditioned response** (or possibly just an ill-mannered Salvation Army worker). "How on earth does any of this apply to compulsive over-eating?" you ask. Well, with the noted exception of Lassie, Rin Tin Tin, and Scooby Doo, most dogs just aren't that bright. They can be easily duped into associating two separate events with the same response, even if one has nothing to do with the other. But as dumb as dogs can be, many are thought to have IQs equivalent to that of a two or three year old child.

In humans, conditioning doesn't wait until you are two or three. Instead, it starts at birth–right from your very first memories. Before you ever had a chance to say, "Hey! Wait a second. Food and feelings don't belong together," you were conditioned to think they were inseparable. In Pavlov's experiment, food was the unconditioned stimulus. In your case, food was the conditioned stimulus. It became associated with feelings and circumstances that should never be connected. Here's how it happened.

You began life as a helpless, defenseless, dependent infant with little awareness of your environment, and even fewer ways to express yourself. But there was one thing that "baby-you" could do–scream your little head off. So whenever you felt the slightest discomfort–WAAAAH! It didn't matter if you were lonely, frightened, tired, or just had gas–you yelled and you were good at it.

Invariably, your mother, father, or caretaker came to your rescue. They were warm, familiar, gentle, and comforting. Things seemed better when they were there. You felt loved. You felt in control. Now even though at this point your mom and dad were way smarter than you, they often couldn't figure out exactly why you were crying. Mom and dad didn't realize that their presence was often all that was needed to comfort you. Instead, they thought this crying stuff required a secret weapon: FORMULA! Each time you wanted their care and support they "rang a bell" called food.

Eventually you grew bigger and could hold your bottle instead of having one held for you. By this time, mom and dad needed to get some sleep. Their idealism aside, they were growing slightly annoyed with all of your yelling. Sooner or later, your parents didn't have as much time as needed to hold you, rock you, or whisper sweet nothings in your ear; but they still had their secret weapon. Sure formula wasn't always the stimulus you wanted, but since it was associated so many times with the calming presence of your parents, you found yourself comforted nonetheless. It was warm, tasty, and full of carbohydrates to increase your serotonin level—formula was pretty darn calming after all.

Over time, the "calming equation" Distress-Parent-Comfort was replaced with Distress-Bottle-Comfort, and included several variations on the theme: Anger-Bottle-Comfort, Loneliness-Bottle-Comfort, Fear-Bottle-Comfort, and so on. During the formative months of your emotional development, food became a "conditioned stimulus" that was associated with comforting your unpleasant feelings.

As you grew out of diapers and into your UnderRoos, this connection between food and comfort was continually reinforced. A scary visit to the doctor was rewarded with a jar full of lollipops awaiting your exit. Cookies and candies passed the time on a boring trip to Aunt So&So's house. If you were a good boy or girl and didn't tip over any mannequins while mommy was shopping, you were treated to ice cream and animal crackers.

Take a moment and think again about your own childhood. I'm sure you can think of plenty of other examples where food became either a pacifier for unwanted feelings of boredom, jealousy, embarrassment, and the likes, or a reward for suppressing your true feelings and "behaving yourself."

But who am I trying to fool? These scenarios take place for all kids, whether or not they grow up to be compulsive overeaters. How can this process nurture the long-lasting maladaptive behaviors seen in compulsive overeaters while the rest of the world passes through this phase? Read on.

Nature Meets Nurture

For most people, conditioned learning is easily "unlearned" (much like high school algebra). You see, Pavlov continued to ring the dinner bell without giving Spot any food. At first the poor dog continued to salivate whenever the familiar bell sounded. But as the days went by, Spot began to slobber less and less. Finally, after realizing that a clanging bell would not satisfy his hunger, Spot stopped salivating to the noise altogether.

Pavlov's dog demonstrated a process known as extinction. No, not the woolly mammoth or saber tooth tiger kind of extinction, but the behavioral kind. **Behavioral extinction** is a phenomenon that occurs when the conditioned event (bell) is continually repeated *without* the unconditioned event (food) until the conditioned response (salivation) first weakens and then disappears. In other words, extinction breaks the unnatural link between two events that were never meant to be connected.

The association between food and emotion undergoes a similar process of extinction. Once formula, cookies, and candy are no longer paired with love and comfort, most children begin to realize that their emotional needs must be met more directly. Over time, food's ability to ease emotional upset gradually decreases and disappears, giving way to healthier patterns of both feeding and feeling. This is the story for most kids. This is not your story!

Sure, extinction was easy for other kids. Their serotonin systems were healthy. HPCs, sugar, and fat never changed their mood or eased their pain, so food never became their emotional crutch. Instead, they went on to develop healthier ways of coping. They learned to be assertive. They learned to relax. They learned to express themselves. Food became food—something to eat—and nothing more.

For you, however, extinction could never take place. The HPCs, sugars, and excess fat you consumed early in life powerfully reinforced your misguided association between food and feeling. Why? Because you were born with the genes of a compulsive overeater, so it is likely you had a subtly deficient serotonin system right from the start. The serotonin spike you got from formula, cookies, and candy actually did comfort you via serotonin's calming properties. These foods made you feel better. They changed your mood and eased your pain. They worked! This positive reinforcement made the bond between feeding and feelings unbreakable. Extinction couldn't possibly occur. So you dealt with your feelings the only way you knew–FOOD!

Chapter 8

Feeding Which Feelings?

A Fall From Grace

Grace seemed like the poster child for recovery. She was abstinent for five years, at her target weight for four years, and was the leader of her overeater's support group. She even appeared on a local TV morning show to share her triumphant recovery from food addiction. But one cold night in December, triumph turned into tragedy–Grace fell off the wagon and relapsed.

Grace's friends first became concerned when she no-showed their Thursday evening Overeaters Anonymous meeting. They tried phoning her, but were greeted only by the computerized chimes of the answering machine. When Grace blew-off work the next morning, everyone assumed the worst. A single female living in a high crime neighborhood– something had to be wrong. After all, the Grace they knew was too responsible to just disappear without notice.

Margaret, Grace's best friend and co-worker, volunteered to swing by Grace's home to check things out. She rang the door bell and knocked loudly, but there was no reply. So with every ounce of courage she could muster, Marge reached into her purse, took out the spare key, and slipped it into the deadbolt's tumblers.

As Marge unlocked the door and stepped into the darkened foyer, she heard the unmistakable sound of television static hissing from Grace's bedroom. Marge ran down the hallway toward the bedroom door, praying she could handle whatever carnage awaited her. But as she entered the room, reality caught her completely by surprise. There was no ransacked furniture or bloody glove. Instead, she saw Grace sitting in bed staring vacantly at the white noise on TV. Strewn beside her were the remnants of her binge: an empty carton of ice cream, one remaining donut from a box of twelve, a half eaten sack of Doritos, and a few surviving crumbs of what was once a loaf of bread.

For a moment, time stood still and neither friend was able to move. Marge was frozen in shock, and Grace was paralyzed with shame and remorse. Grace finally broke the long silence. Raising her sullen eyes, a single tear rolled down her cheek. She looked at Marge and softly pleaded, "Help me."

Help arrived under an umbrella of love and support as Grace's support group rallied to her side. They knew Grace's inner strength and devotion would guide her back into recovery, but they couldn't help wondering, "Why did she relapse after five binge-free years? Could she have prevented this? Could the same thing happen to us?"

What shattered Grace's recovery? Each of her friends had their own hypothesis. There was the "grassy knoll," or conspiracy theory: Grace unwittingly ate something with sugar in it and triggered the disease (much like the alcoholic who relapses after rinsing with Listerine). Then there was the genetic theory: some hereditary flaw produced a system-wide serotonin shutdown, forcing Grace to self-medicate with binge food. There were other theories as well–all very creative–all very biologic–and all very wrong!

I'm not suggesting that biology doesn't play a role in relapse; you know I would never do that. Inadvertently eating HPCs, sugar, or excess fat, modifying The Menu For Life, or neglecting to treat a mood disorder can all trigger a physiologic drive to binge. Yet for Grace, and for many other compulsive overeaters, there is no chemical, gene, or food to blame when abandoning abstinence. Instead, relapse begins with a single overpowering emotion. Because whether it's your first food memory or the millionth time you've binged, feeding your feelings starts with just that–feelings!

Which feelings do you feed? Well, that depends on you and the life you lead. Any emotion (even joy) can stoke the fires of your disease. But chances are, the real flames of your compulsive overeating are fueled by one of these six feelings:

Depression	Anger	Powerlessness
Shame	Loneliness	Fear

Whether your own personal "calming equation" is Shame-Food-Comfort, Loneliness-Food-Comfort, Depression-Food-Comfort, or some combination thereof, remains to be seen. But one thing is clear. Food has been feeding your feelings over, and over, and over again.

With this in mind, let's take a closer look at each of these feelings and their relationship to compulsive overeating. We've already covered depression in depth, so let's review the other five, starting with the feeling that Grace fed–anger–pure unadulterated white hot rage.

Anger

Grace had the kind of mother that only a daughter could love. Well, maybe not love, but at least tolerate. Okay, maybe tolerate is a bit too kind. To be perfectly honest, Grace couldn't stand her mother–nobody could.

Nothing was good enough for Grace's mom, especially

Grace. When Grace placed second in the state-wide spelling bee, her mom didn't congratulate her. Instead, she scolded Grace in front of a room full of strangers for misspelling "ostentatious." At every pivotal juncture in Grace's childhood, her mom was there to belittle and rebuke her. Perhaps Grace could have weathered this constant barrage of criticism if her mom had practiced the perfection that she preached. But in reality, Grace's mother was nothing more than a drifter–drifting from husband to husband, job to job, and bar to bar. Her hypocrisy was enough to infuriate Ghandi, but not Grace.

Grace learned at an early age not to express anger. The few times Grace challenged her mother's scornful outbursts, she received a swift backhand to the face. So given the choice between emotional or physical abuse, Grace made an understandable decision–accept the faultfinding, avoid the battering, and swallow anger at all costs. But anger was a bitter pill to swallow, and the adage "a spoonful of sugar helps the medicine go down," became Grace's motto. Bingeing sweetened anger's sour taste. It was the only way she knew to stomach her rage and survive.

Grace didn't think about serotonin, tryptophan, or genetics as her compulsive overeating grew worse. She thought only about survival and feeding the anger she wasn't allowed to feel. When Grace finally realized that her eating was out of control, she welcomed abstinence, yet ignored her anger. She never learned to face her wrath and express it in an appropriate manner. Instead, she walled off her anger even further by severing all ties with her mother. As a result, Grace's recovery was built like the straw house in the *Three Little Pigs*. It was fully functional (allowing her to maintain a 60 pound weight loss) but easily blown over by the Big Bad Wolf. Five years into recovery, the Big Bad Wolf came huffing and puffing at Grace's doorstep–Mother paid a visit.

Grace's mother arrived unexpectedly, under the pretense of paying a friendly visit to her long lost daughter. In truth, she just walked out on husband number six and needed a place to stay. It didn't take her long to start nitpicking.

"Grace", she said, "Why don't you live in a better neighborhood? Can't you afford a more comfortable guest bed? Are you still hanging around with those other fatsos? You know, maybe if you fixed up your hair you could catch yourself a husband."

Grace's anger grew with each poisonous comment. At first it simmered, then it rolled to a raging boil. By the time her mother left, only two days later, the fires of Grace's anger were so hot that she was on the verge of an emotional meltdown. Five years of abstinence hadn't taught Grace a thing about venting the anger that burned within her. So she cooled off the only way she knew—ice cream, then donuts, then chips, until her fury was snuffed out like a blanket smothering a flame. In that moment, Grace didn't give a darn about abstinence or recovery. All she cared about was easing her pain.

How much do you have in common with Grace? Probably more than you realize. After all, how many times in your own life were you told, "If you don't have anything nice to say, then don't say anything at all." Most of us are taught that anger is bad, and that people who show their anger are somehow dangerous. Grace learned this the hard way. Maybe you did too.

Or perhaps just the opposite occurred. Maybe there was too much anger in your home, and fighting was your only mode of communication. Not surprisingly, there are some compulsive overeaters whose only emotion is anger. Take Jamie for instance.

Jamie's childhood wasn't all that different from Grace's. She too was raised in an emotionally and physically abusive home. But whereas Grace chose to stuff down her anger, Jamie wore hers like a thick winter shawl. She wrapped herself in anger until it enveloped the very essence of her being. Jamie didn't care about the consequences of her anger. She acted out whenever, wherever, and toward whomever she wanted, including herself.

How did Jamie's overeating fit into this? Have you ever

heard someone say, "I'll show you. I'll hurt myself, and then you'll be sorry." Well, despite Jamie's outward anger, she still had an inner need for love and affection. Since Jamie's needs were never fulfilled by her parents, she found another source—food. For Jamie, bingeing served a dual purpose. It was her only source of comfort, and it also gave her another way to act out her anger (bingeing is quite self-destructive).

So how about you? Are you like Grace; never showing anger, but eating it away? Or are you more like Jamie; communicating only with anger, even to the point of acting out your anger with food? When was the last time anger was the feeling that you fed?

Powerlessness

Powerlessness can be defined in a variety of ways. Most of us think of powerlessness as having lost all control. Others describe it as being compelled to do something that they desperately don't want to do. But I'll bet only Sally thinks of powerlessness as having a face, a body, and a name: Henry.

Sally's relationship with her stepfather, Henry, nearly destroyed her. His control over her was all encompassing, right down to the food she ate. In fact, Sally's first food memory is of Henry padlocking the refrigerator door so she wouldn't get into "his food." Meanwhile, Henry had *carte blanche* over the kitchen. Sally remembers him building huge roast beef sandwiches on hard salted rolls, then eating them right in front of her. She still feels the hurt and rejection these memories evoke. "Why could Henry have whatever he wanted?" she wondered, and "Why did everything I eat require Henry's approval?"

The rest of Sally's childhood memories are just as painful. Her mother was an alcoholic, and Henry had several run-ins with the law. As a family, they moved seven times in six years. Sometimes, Sally wouldn't even know they were moving until the day it happened. With each move, Sally was forced to change schools, friends, and homes. Only one thing was certain–no matter where Sally moved, there was always a padlock in the kitchen. These memories still haunt Sally. They were the beginning of her struggles–her struggle with power, her struggle with control, and her struggle with food.

By the time the 8th grade rolled around, Sally had left behind all of her friends but one–food! Since she still wasn't allowed to eat without Henry's permission, Sally became an expert at sneaking food. She ate quickly. That way, no one realized just how much she truly ate. When dinner was finished, Sally would volunteer to clean the dishes, then raid the leftovers from her family's plates. She even went so far as to steal and copy the key to Henry's infamous padlock.

Every time Sally successfully "ate without permission," she felt more powerful. It was like she was getting one over on Henry, whom she hated. To Sally, being able to eat whatever and whenever she wanted became proof that she, and not Henry, had control over her life.

Food became her obsession. She ate big and she ate often. Why? Because she was in control. Cookies became her best friend. It didn't matter if they were fresh, stale, or even frozen; she ate them, again, and again, and again. Why? Because she was in control. Her binges lasted for hours, and sometimes days. Why? Because she was in control. She controlled food. She controlled life!

It wasn't until several years and 244 pounds later that Sally realized how out of control her life had truly become. Henry was long gone, but another master ruled her–food! Sally endured weight gain, marital strife, and failing health all in the name of food. It called out her name, and she submitted to its every whim. Sally wasn't in control–food was, and that felt lousy.

Face it, Sally isn't alone. Powerlessness stinks. To make matters worse, feeling powerless in one area of life, usually leads to hyper-control over everything else. This is especially true for compulsive overeaters. If you aren't a control freak, then I'm sure you know people who are. They are the know-it-alls of absolutely everything. Having control makes them feel safe, important, and secure.

So why do so many compulsive overeaters have issues with control? Probably because they recognize, on some subconscious level, that they really have no control at all. Not only are they powerless over such things as who their parents are or how they were raised, they don't even have control over the amount of food they consume. Compulsive overeaters are powerless over food!

Recognizing your powerlessness is the first step in every twelve-step recovery program. It's also vital to breaking the R.U.T. of compulsive overeating. Unfortunately, it's difficult for others to understand what you are going through. They may think, "How can someone be powerless over a God-given necessity? Food can't be addictive, after all, it's not a drug." Wrong! Food is a drug. It can be as addictive as alcohol, cocaine, or gambling. Once you start, it's difficult to stop.

Shame

Shame is truly one of the most distressing feelings. Webster's defines shame as: "a painful emotion caused by a strong sense of guilt, embarrassment, unworthiness, or disgrace." Notice that Webster's uses the word "guilt" to define shame. But the first thing you need to know about shame is that it's really not the same as guilt.

Guilt is feeling badly about something you said, did, or thought. You feel guilt as a result of an action. Shame, on the other hand, is feeling badly about who you are. It is a core feeling that tells you, "I am not a good person."

If little Johnny pilfers a candy bar from the Mini-Mart, you want him to feel guilty about stealing it. Hopefully guilt will cause him to confess, or at least never repeat the act. You should not, however, want Johnny to feel shame, or think he's a terrible person because he made a single mistake. There's a big difference in semantics. It's the difference between, "You did something bad," and, "You are bad."

Many compulsive overeaters believe they are bad people. They don't feel worthy enough to have their needs met. Some don't even believe they have a right to live. Their shame is so paralyzing that even when they find the road to recovery, many feel too undeserving to travel it.

Take Mary for instance. She was programmed at an early age to feel shame. Her parents were rigid perfectionists. "It's my way or the highway," was the rule of the house, and Mary's parents ruled with an iron fist. When Mary wasn't toilet trained by age two, her parents berated her. When she wanted to learn how to play guitar, they refused and forced her to take piano lessons. When she asked permission to perm her hair, the answer was a resounding, "No! We won't let any curly haired slut live in our house." Whatever Mary longed for, it was denied. The message she received was loud and clear: "Your wants are wrong, your needs are wrong, and Mary, you are wrong."

Over the years, Mary's self-worth disintegrated. In its place stood shame. Shame followed Mary like a shadow, growing in the morning sun until it towered high above her. She became ashamed of her wants, so she wanted nothing. She became ashamed of her needs, so she asked for nothing. She became ashamed of herself, so she felt like nothing. Shame burned a hole in the very center of Mary's soul.

All of us have wants and needs. Mary was no different, except that her needs were never met. So what did she do? She found a substitute–FOOD! No matter where she went, how she looked, or how she felt, food was there for Mary. Food met her needs and gave her comfort without ever shaming her. Food and compulsive overeating filled the hole in Mary's soul.

But there's another side of shame to compulsive overeating that many people prefer not to mention. It's the shame the disease brings. The shame of being 270 pounds–the shame you feel when you're buying a bunch of junk food and the checkout person shakes his/her head in disgust–the shame of being fat. Compulsive overeating takes shame and twists it into a vicious circle. At least that's what happened to Anna.

Let's pick up Anna's story in the middle of her disease. She was 26 years old, newly married, weighed 265 pounds, and was just hired as an executive secretary for a local law firm. Unfortunately, Anna had only one appropriate work outfit. So she did what any of us would do. She went shopping. Anna still recalls the shame of it all:

> It was so disappointing. I tried on every business suit in the store. I didn't care about color or style, I just wanted something big enough to fit me—but nothing did. I was so ashamed of my body that I actually hid when I saw my old friend Patty. I didn't want her to see me looking for "fat people" clothes.
>
> My frustration led me to a nearby restaurant where I downed a double cheeseburger, large fries, and a jumbo hot fudge sundae. I felt so angry, hopeless, and shameful about myself. Eating was the only way I knew to feel better. I didn't mean to eat that much. As a matter of fact, when the waitress brought me the sundae, I looked at how big it was and thought, 'I can't eat all this, it's too big—and then it was gone.

That's the vicious circle of compulsive overeating. Feeling shame about who you are and how you look; then eating away the shame because you don't know what else to do with it.

Loneliness

Bottom line—food is your friend, your buddy, and your confidant. Food doesn't talk back, hit, or ridicule you in any way. Food loves you unconditionally. It's always there for you. Always!

You saw how food can fill the hole in your soul, now see how it fills the emptiness within you. The truth is, compulsive overeaters are lonely people. Somewhere along the line, you were denied the love and attention you needed to feel whole. So food filled the void. Since many compulsive overeaters were raised in the void of an alcoholic home, let's take a look at such a family and the feelings that were fed.

Albert had many roles in life: loving husband, devoted father, school principal, and alcoholic. No, Albert wasn't the falling-down-gutter-drunk that most of us mistakenly picture. In fact, he was much like the other twenty million alcoholics nationwide. He held a good job, provided for his family, and was generally a great guy to be around—as long as he was sober. Unfortunately he wasn't sober very often. Every night after work, and throughout the weekend, Albert would drink himself into oblivion. With each drink he was transformed. Sober Albert, the great guy, became Drunk Albert, the tyrant. And no one experienced more of Albert's tyranny and the loneliness it created than his only son, Milton

Milton never had many friends, though it wasn't for lack of effort or desire. Sure, Milton was shy, not particularly coordinated, and a little pudgy, but the main reason for his solitude was Albert's drunkenness. Milton tells it this way:

> It was tough enough making friends with dad being the principal, and thanks to his drunken antics, I sure couldn't keep any. I remember one time when a new kid moved in down the street and I tried to become his friend. We were playing cops and robbers, and I invited him to my house for some lemonade. Well, we were a little dirty and ended up tracking a few flecks of mud onto the kitchen floor. Dad was bombed and went berserk. He screamed bloody murder. It was the most embarrassing moment of my life, and it scared the daylights out of my friend. After that day, he didn't play with me anymore and I never invited anyone into my home again.

From that day on, Milton was alone. His dad was too drunk to offer any support, and his mom was so overwhelmed by Albert's behavior that she too was emotionally unavailable. So Milton found a new playmate—food. Milton describes it like this:

Food was the only friend I could count on. I thought about it twenty four hours a day. As soon as I got home from school, I'd run to the refrigerator and say hello to my buddies—Mrs. Butterworth, Dolly Madison, and Little Debbie. I'd eat all the junk I could cram down my throat. Other kids would be outside playing, but I knew I couldn't join them. Dad would somehow see to that, so I just stayed inside with my food and ate the loneliness away.

Loneliness wasn't just a feeling Milton fed, it was also a consequence of his addiction. Compulsive overeating is a disease of isolation. Milton didn't binge in front of others and neither do you. After all, what would people think if they saw how much you really ate? My guess is that you binge in secret and solitude. Most of the time you binge alone. Like Milton, food may be your only friend.

Fear

"The only thing we have to fear, is fear itself." John F. Kennedy understood the power of fear as he spoke those famous words. Fear destroys from within. It's a cancer that cripples the spirit.

Meet Pam. At first glance you would never guess that fear rules her thoughts and deeds. She doesn't stammer, sweat, or tremble. In fact, Pam can look you straight in the eye and smile with an air of complete confidence. But get to know Pam, and you'll quickly learn her assuredness is nothing more than a facade: a mask that shrouds the face of fear.

Pam wasn't raised in chaos, abuse, or neglect like so many other compulsive overeaters. In fact, her parents were quite loving. Pam's mother, Joyce, was a kind and caring homemaker. Her father, Steve, was a devoted and respected sheriff in a town so quiet it's called Serene, Indiana. Yet on the eve of Pam's eighth birthday, a single shot from a 22 caliber handgun broke that silence and shattered Pam's nerves.

The call came over the dispatch, "Domestic disturbance

at 314 Hatcher Street. Officer assistance requested." Steve responded. He could hear a young women screaming as he approached the door, identified himself, and saw the woman's husband give her one last slap to the face. But as Steve entered the home, the disputing lovers quickly composed themselves and appeared quite cooperative. The husband smiled broadly and explained that the whole incident was just a simple misunderstanding between a man and his wife. But somehow, a simple misunderstanding didn't explain the blackened eye and bloodied lip worn by his battered spouse. Steve heard the woman's cries, saw her bruises, and witnessed the assault. The law was clear. The man had battered his wife, and he was going to jail.

The arrest went smoothly. The man offered no resistance; he placed his hands behind his back and was cuffed without incident. It wasn't until they were heading toward the patrol car that trouble ensued. In an action so unexpected that it defied all logic, the young woman ran down the stairs, brandished a pistol, and yelled, "You're not taking my baby to jail." With that, she aimed and fired right through Steve's shoulder.

It was the proverbial "flesh wound." Steve was fine. Of course Pam didn't know this when Joyce awakened her and told her that her father was shot. All the way to the hospital Pam feared the worst. "Dad's dead," she thought, "They just want to tell me in person in case I fall apart." When she saw her father sitting up in bed, conversing happily with some fellow cops, Pam dropped to her knees and sobbed with relief; but she couldn't stop thinking, "Sure he's fine this time, but what about tomorrow?" Fear had planted it's seed, taken root, and begun to grow.

Pam was just a kid and had no idea how to handle her fear. She refused to talk about it, as if voicing her concern would somehow doom her father. Instead, as Pam explains, she calmed her fear with food:

> I remember watching an old TV western where the gunslinger slammed a shot of bourbon to quiet his nerves before facing his enemies in battle. Well, I

know this sounds silly, but I went home that night, poured myself a short glass of Koolaid, and downed shot after shot until I was blissfully wired on tropical punch. From that night on, when I feared, I binged. Every time dad left for work, I thought it would be the last time I'd see him alive. So I feared, and I binged. I learned to avoid conflict at all costs, fearing the same unpredictable forces that caught my father by surprise. Instead, I acted aloof, ignoring my wants and needs; and I feared, and I binged. I had lots of boyfriends, but none of them were serious. I wouldn't allow myself to get involved. I'd become prissy and break things off, but really I was afraid of losing them. So once again, I feared, I binged, and I grew bigger and bigger, and bigger."

Fear, more than any other emotion, feeds the addictive cycle of compulsive overeating. Even skeptics who scoff at the concept of food addiction, begrudgingly admit that they too are inclined to moments of dietary indiscretion when feeling anxious and stressed. Of course it never occurs to them that their momentary lapse in self-restraint actually triggered a release in opioids and serotonin that helped calm their fears. They just write it off as a fleeting act of fancy, but you know better. Fear gnaws at your psyche. Fear devours your will. Fear consumes—and so do you!

The Formula For Recovery

So what's the answer to all of this feelings stuff? How can you deal with fear, anger, loneliness and the likes? Express yourself! That's how. Don't ignore your feelings. Abstinence is only half the formula you need to overcome compulsive overeating. Here's the entire equation:

ABSTINENT FEEDING + EXPRESSIVE FEELING =
           (BIOLOGY)   (PSYCHOLOGY)

RECOVERY!

Okay, so maybe it's not as earth shattering as $E=MC^2$, but it's a heck of a lot more practical. Compulsive overeaters use binge food to numb their feelings. Grace numbed her anger, Milton numbed his loneliness, and Mary numbed her shame. Do you know what you've been numbing? Well, you'll soon find out.

Abstinence removes your emotional novocaine, so it's only natural for feelings to resurface. Until you learn to deal with these emotions, without walling them off, recovery can never be complete. With this in mind, let's look at the other half of the Recovery Equation: **Expressive Feeling** and the psychological treatment of compulsive overeating.

Chapter 9

Treating Overeating
Part II

Expressive Feelings

Express yourself. Express your feelings. That's the missing half of your recovery equation. Of course this is easier said than done. After all, you've been stuffing feelings down your throat for a very long time. Some of them are probably stuck there. But once you stop numbing your mood with food, your emotional Novocaine will quickly wear off and dormant feelings will soon awaken. Jamie, for example, spent the first few days of abstinence crying. Twenty-two years of tears were packed into her soul when she unlocked the flood gates of recovery. Grace wasn't much different. A lifetime of repressed anger erupted into three days of foot-stomping temper tantrums. Who knows what feelings might emerge in your first days of abstinence.

So why on earth would you possibly want to express

some of the rotten hurtful feelings you've been feeding? The answer is simple. You have to. It's the only way to be true to yourself and to your recovery. Besides, all feelings, whether they are good, bad, happy, or sad, are natural, healthy, God-given emotions. It's okay to feel them, even if some of them are hurtful. Just think of them as small potholes on your road to recovery.

I realize that this may seem a little scary at first. Many compulsive overeaters fear they will lose control if they start expressing their true feelings. But it doesn't work that way. It never has and it never will. In fact, once you face your feelings and accept them as valid, food will no longer rule you. You will!

So then, how do you best express your feelings after a lifetime of feeding them? Assert yourself, affirm yourself, and love yourself. That's how. The next few pages will assist you in this endeavor by giving you several practical exercises to improve your communication skills, lift your self-esteem, and boost your body image.

Assert Yourself

Some aspects of recovery are amazingly simple. Unfortunately, compulsive overeaters don't buy simple. They think, "How can this lifelong obsession and torture possibly have simple answers?" Well it can, and one of them is called *assertiveness*.

Assertiveness is the ability to stand up for your rights while respecting the rights of others. Assertiveness is the key to effective communication, interpersonal growth, openness, and honesty. It is without a doubt the most important step you can take toward expressive feelings. Assertiveness is many things, but it is nothing without the two fundamentals contained within its definition: rights and respect.

RIGHTS

Know your rights! All too often compulsive overeaters take their own needs for granted. They sacrifice feelings in order to keep an elusive peace, and communicate in a **passive** style that undermines all hope for assertiveness. Here is a typical example:

Imagine that Betty the Binger just arrived home from work. It was a lousy day at the office, and she needs to talk about her troubles with her husband, Marc. Now Marc had a rough day as well, but he prefers to unwind by reading the evening paper. Let's look at the passive conversation that takes place between these two. Pay attention to both their verbal and nonverbal language.

Betty
Verbal: You wouldn't believe the miserable day I had.
Nonverbal: Nervous, voice timid, poor eye contact.

Marc
Verbal: Huh? Oh, sounds pretty bad, but can we talk later? I'm right in the middle of Ann Landers.
Nonverbal: Reading the paper, not looking up.

Betty
Verbal: Okay, we'll talk later.
Nonverbal: Voice soft, eyes and head down, reaching for the coffee cake.

Marc
Verbal: Yeah, no problem.
Nonverbal: Keeps reading paper.

This doesn't sound too bad, does it? Betty didn't get what she wanted, but relationships are about compromise, right? Well, yes they are; however, difficulties arise when the passive party has a need that isn't fulfilled because it isn't expressed. Let's face facts. Marc isn't a mind reader, and neither is your spouse, boss, family, or friends. If you don't say what you need, you can bet you won't get what you need. Herein lies the problem with passive communication. You walk away angry and frustrated because, once again, you didn't get your needs met. The anger from one situation may not be overwhelming or unmanageable, but pile it on top of the last twenty-five unmet needs and you are close to an uncontrollable rage–a rage that can only be calmed by yet another binge. Remember, you must learn to verbally express yourself if your needs are to be met. That's effective communication. That's your right.

Exercise 1: The constitution grants you certain inalienable rights such as life, liberty, and the pursuit of happiness. But none of this means peanuts if you don't grant yourself the same privilege. Step 1 in assertiveness training is to recognize and champion your rights as a person. Copy the following list and keep it with you. These are your rights:

I have the right to...

Be myself
Feel and express anger
Feel and express sadness
Make mistakes
Have my own opinion
Make my needs as important as the needs of others
Change my mind
Ask for help and compassion
Take pride in myself and my accomplishments
Say "No" without feeling selfish
Say "I don't know" without feeling stupid
Say "I disagree" without feeling guilt
Be heard
Grow
Love
Learn

RESPECT

Let's get one thing straight. Assertiveness is not about always getting your way, nor is it about coercion, manipulation, or failure to compromise. Assertiveness is all about mutual respect–respect for yourself, and respect for others. Many compulsive overeaters deny themselves respect when they fall into the hole of passive communication; but an even deadlier hole exists–the hole of **aggressive** communication. Let's take a look at the same scenario with Betty and Marc that now turns aggressive.

<u>Betty</u>
Verbal: You wouldn't believe the miserable day I had.
Nonverbal: Scowling, voice firm, staring at Marc.

<u>Marc</u>
Verbal: Huh? Oh, sounds pretty bad, but can we talk later? I'm right in the middle of Ann Landers.
Nonverbal: Reading the paper, not looking up.
(Notice that Marc is still reacting the same as in the passive scenario.)

<u>Betty</u>
Verbal: I can't believe you! All you do is sit in that stupid chair, you lazy slob. I needed to talk to you, but now I have nothing to say.
Nonverbal: Voice enraged, towering over Marc, shaking her finger at him.

<u>Marc</u>
Verbal: What did I do?
Nonverbal: Picks up his paper and retreats to the bedroom.

Notice that in this scene, Betty was quick to react with the anger that typifies aggressive communication. Even though she managed to state her need, the message was lost in a flurry of caustic remarks and shaking fingers. Marc never heard her need. All he heard was her rage.

Think for a moment about your own response when someone yells at you. The normal reaction is to either withdraw, as Marc did, or fight back. Either way, the message is lost. In the end, the result is no different than passive communication. Your needs (and Betty's) still aren't met.

Exercise 2: Sooner or later, someone, somewhere is going to make your blood boil. It's only human to feel anger, but don't let anger get the best of you. Give yourself a "time-out."

You have heard of the exercise of counting to 10 before saying anything in haste. Well forget about it! Ten seconds is barely enough time to take a deep breath, let alone return you to your senses. Whenever you see yourself heading toward aggressive communication, take at least a two-minute break to regain your composure. Leave the room, walk around the yard; heck, walk all the way to Florida if you have to. Just do whatever it takes to calm down, then return and state your needs assertively. So before you say something hurtful, take a time-out, because you can never take time back.

ASSERTIVENESS 101

Here it is. The key to effective communication:

> I feel _____
> When you _____
> And I prefer _____

It's amazing! These three little fill-in-the-blank phrases will give you what you need–assertiveness–a surefire way to confidently express your needs without violating the rights of others. Let's take a closer look at each of these lines.

I feel _____

Claim them and name them! Feelings, that is. Assertiveness starts by taking ownership of your feelings with the use of the word "I." Claiming your feelings as your own, eliminates the opportunity for the receiver to become defensive. You aren't blaming him/her for your feelings as you do with a "You make me feel" statement. Instead you acknowledge that the feelings are yours to control. You choose them. You claim them.

That brings us to the word "feel." Expressive feelings

just don't happen *unless you express a feeling*! The "I feel" statement must always be followed by a feeling, *not* a thought. For example, "I feel angry," "I feel tired," or "I feel frustrated" are all perfectly appropriate examples of an "I feel" statement. On the other hand, saying, "I feel you are a big jerk," is completely inappropriate and sabotages your intention to be assertive. There's no feeling stated. It's just an accusatory statement with the words "I feel" thrown in to cover up a nasty remark.

Exercise 3: How are you feeling today? Maybe you aren't quite sure. Maybe you've been feeding your feelings for so long that you are completely out of touch with your true emotions. So take a look at the following list of feelings:

Exhausted	Embarrassed
Overwhelmed	Mischievous
Confused	Happy
Hopeful	Shy
Ecstatic	Lonely
Guilty	Disgusted
Lovestruck	Confident
Suspicious	Frightened
Jealous	Sad
Angry	Enraged
Bored	Shocked
Hysterical	Ashamed
Surprised	Hurt
Frustrated	Cautious
Anxious	Smug

Next, write several short sentences about a time in your life when you experienced each of these feelings. If there are some you can't recall ever feeling, put a star beside them. Sometimes the "unfelt" feelings are the ones that binge food hides from you. Return to the list after 90 days of abstinence and repeat this exercise. See if you can reacquaint yourself with these feelings and the world of emotion you may have missed.

When you _____

This statement pinpoints the behavior that prompts you to express your feelings. It must be as specific and nonjudgmental as possible. "I feel frustrated when you <u>write a check without annotating it in our checkbook</u>," or "I feel hurt when you <u>tell people secrets I've told you</u>," are both perfect examples of pinpointing a specific behavior. On the other hand, saying, "I feel frustrated when you <u>mess everything up</u>," is far too general to be of value. Likewise, saying something like, "I feel hurt when you <u>don't take me seriously</u>," judges another's behavior. It doesn't pinpoint it. When you generalize or judge, you invite defensiveness and prevent direct and healthy communication.

And I prefer_____

Here's your big chance to state your needs. This doesn't guarantee you'll always get your way, but at least it puts all the cards on the table. Remember, the goal of effective communication is to express your needs and feelings, not force someone else to submit to your every whim. That will never happen. Of course there are a couple of ways to increase your odds.

First, make sure you are stating a "need" and not a "want." Asking for affection is one thing, but asking for a red Ferrari with Corinthian leather seats just won't cut it. Secondly, make your request clear and concrete. For example, "I feel hurt when you tell people our secrets and I prefer <u>you keep in confidence anything I tell you unless you have my permission to share it.</u>" Notice that this request is very specific, but still allows room for compromise. You aren't demanding a vow of silence. You are just asking the other person to check with you before sharing personal matters. Saying anything less could lead to the black hole of communication: that never ending conversation where no one is heard, and no one gets their needs met. For example, "I feel hurt when you tell people our secrets and I prefer you <u>respect my privacy</u>." That's far too vague. A likely response would be, "But honey, I do respect your privacy. It's not like I barge in on you when you're in the bathroom." At that point, get the ladder and start climbing your way out of the black hole.

I feel ___when you ___and I would prefer ___. It's really that simple. But assertiveness isn't always rainbows and butterflies. It takes practice and patience. The traps of passive and aggressive communication are hard habits to break; and don't expect anyone else to help you break them. After all, people are used to you not getting your needs met. They like it that way. It makes it much easier for them to get their needs met if they don't have to consider yours. Too bad! Because now you know how to communicate effectively, express your feelings, and state your needs. Now you can be assertive–just like Betty.

Betty
Verbal: You wouldn't believe the miserable day I had.
Nonverbal: Voice calm, looking at Marc.

Marc
Verbal: Huh? Oh, sounds pretty bad, but can we talk later? I'm right in the middle of Ann Landers.
Nonverbal: Reading the paper, not looking up.

Betty
Verbal: I feel ignored when you read the paper while I'm speaking, and I would prefer that you spend five minutes talking with me before you continue.
Nonverbal: Voice calm, sitting level with Marc, good eye contact continues.

Marc
Verbal: I'm sorry Honey. I didn't realize how important this was to you.
Nonverbal: Puts down paper and begins to listen attentively.
(and they lived happily ever after!)

Affirm Yourself

Self-esteem! It's the hottest topic in town. Everybody is talking about it, and they all say it's lacking. It's as though the gurus of pop psychology have pulled out our emotional dipsticks and convinced us that we are all running a quart low. But just what is this self-esteem stuff?

Actually, self-esteem is easy to define: it's *your* thoughts and feelings about yourself. Notice that it has absolutely nothing to do with what anyone else thinks of you. Of course there was a time, when you were still too young to think on your own, that other people's thoughts and statements did contribute to your sense of self. But that's no longer the case! You are grown now and responsible for shaping your own self-esteem. The negative messages you have in your head, such as, "I'm not good enough," "I'm fat and lazy," or "I never do anything right," may have been put there by somebody else, but now you are empowered to change those thoughts. So instead of focusing on why your self-esteem is low, let's begin to work on raising it.

Human nature is such that if I told you over and over again, "You are a failure," you would soon begin to think of yourself as a failure, regardless of your past successes. Intellectually, you may know this isn't true, but on an emotional level, it would become so real that eventually you would start giving yourself the same message: "I am a failure." Now this wouldn't be a very nice thing to say to yourself, but my guess is, like most compulsive overeaters, you have somehow learned to give yourself dozens of these self-defeating messages. Messages that whittled away your confidence and lowered your self-esteem. Therefore, the first step toward boosting your self-esteem is learning to recognize these negative messages, so you can begin to rewrite them in a positive way.

Exercise 4: Spend one day paying attention to the negative messages you give yourself. Tuck a piece of paper in your pocket and every time you think or say something negative about yourself, write it down. Notice throughout the day how many different negative thoughts you have about yourself and how many times you repeat them. Sometimes these thoughts will be pretty extensive, such as, "I'm so fat. Just look at my thighs. I can't believe how big I'm getting. I know people are staring at me." Yet as extensive as these thoughts may be, try to break them down into five or six simple word statements that are easy to manage. Eventually your list will look something like this:

Negative Self Thoughts	How Many Times
I am not good enough.	3
I am not a good spouse.	2
I am slow.	3
I am not lovable.	1
I am stubborn.	2
I am not a good employee.	2

At the end of the day, review your list, and ask yourself this question: Would I ever say these awful things to my enemies, let alone my friends? My guess is that you will answer, "No!"

My point is this: If you treat yourself as nice as you treat your best friends, then you are well on your way to higher self-esteem.

Exercise 5: On a separate piece of paper, create two columns. Rewrite your negative comments in the left-hand column. Next, in the right-hand column, create a list of positive affirmations that directly counters each negative thought. It should look something like this:

Negative Self-Thoughts	Positive Affirmation
I am not good enough.	I am good enough.
I am not a good spouse.	I am a wonderful spouse.

I am slow.	I am purposeful.
I am not lovable.	I am lovable.
I am stubborn.	I am independent.
I am not a good employee.	I am a good employee.

Now comes the hard part. You have to change the tape in your head that plays negative self-thoughts, to one that plays positive affirmations. Wouldn't it be great if someone could press the eject button on your forehead, take out the old tape, and put in a new one? Well sorry, it just doesn't work that way. Only you can change the contents of your tape; and the best way to make this change is to repeat your positive affirmations twice as often as your negative ones.

For example, I'm sure you have heard of the silly little exercise where you stand in front of the mirror, look yourself straight in the eye, and say nice things about yourself. Well, it may be silly but it works, so do it!

Write your positive affirmations on a sheet of paper, then recite them in your car, while brushing your teeth, or at your desk. Say them anywhere and everywhere. Remember, you alone have the power to change your self-esteem. If you sit around just hoping to feel better, you will die waiting–possibly of the physical consequences of compulsive overeating. It's up to you. Do the work and change your tape!

Love Yourself

Mirror, mirror on the wall, who's the fairest of them all?

When was the last time you gazed at your own reflection, asked yourself this question, and answered, "It's me. I'm the fairest of them all." Last week? Last month? Last century? Probably never. In fact, if you are like most compulsive overeaters, you've adapted a completely twisted version of the Evil Queen's incantation. One that goes like this:

Scale, scale on the floor, please don't tell me I weigh more.

Self-hatred is a by-product of food addiction. It results in the dreaded "too syndrome." I'm too fat–too hippy–too flat chested. It's too this and too that, until you develop a total distortion of your body image. In fact, no matter what you weigh, you think of yourself as being heavier than ever. Years of eating in an uncontrollable manner has created a body image that's equally out of control. If you aren't convinced, then try the following exercises to see whether you too are part of this "too syndrome."

Exercise 6: Take a piece of blank paper. Without looking in the mirror, draw a picture of yourself. After you've finished, turn the paper over and go to a full length mirror. Now draw a picture of what you see in the mirror. Compare the two pictures. Chances are, the picture you initially drew is distorted in comparison to your actual image. Hopefully this will allow you to see some of the distortions that most compulsive overeaters have toward their bodies. Hold on to these pictures; after 90 days of abstinence, do the exercise again and notice the difference (not in your body, but in your perception of your body).

Exercise 7: For this exercise you'll need the help of a very good friend. Stand in front of a full length mirror. Beginning at the top of your head, describe your body to your friend. Be as descriptive as possible. For example, "I have thin brunette hair with a hint of gray and a touch of Irish red highlights." Whatever you see, call it like it is. After you've completed your description, have your friend describe what he/she sees. After your friend describes your body, look in the mirror and ask yourself these questions:

1. Am I comfortable looking at myself? Why or why not?

2. What did I feel when my friend was describing my body?

3. How differently did I see myself compared to how my friend saw me?

Don't be surprised by the distortion of your self-image. It's just another symptom of the disease—a form of "stinking-thinking" that's common to all eating disorders. The way you view your body depends not on facts like, size, shape or weight, but on feelings. You feel bad, therefore you look bad. Well stop beating yourself up! It's time to heal. It's time to love yourself.

As you continue the process of emotional recovery, you'll need to let go of your old, warped views and learn to accept yourself. Of course, breaking through this self-distortion isn't always easy; especially when the Calvin Kleins of the world are constantly presenting rail thin beauty as the cultural ideal. But trust that The Menu For Life will take you and your body exactly where you need to be. More importantly, realize that you are a summation of body, mind, and spirit that can't be measured in pounds or inches. Try adding this to your list of positive affirmations:

I am beautiful on the inside and outside.

Say it twenty times a day if you can. Say it until you believe it. Say it until you can gaze at your reflection and say with confidence:

I am the fairest of them all.

No Man is an Island

Want some good news? You now have almost all the tools needed to begin your emotional recovery...**Hip-Hip-Hooray**! Want some even better news? There's still one more exercise left for you to do...hip-hip-hooray. Hey, that's not very enthusiastic. Okay, okay, so maybe these exercises do seem silly, but they work, and this one will too. So without further delay, let's bring on the ultimate challenge: your final exercise!

Exercise 8: Put down this wonderful book, go find a big-screen TV and pick it up over your head. That's right, lift it way up high. Twirl it around a few times.

Maybe throw it in the air like a pizza. What? What's wrong? What do you mean it's too tough an exercise to do by yourself? Oh, I'm sorry. I didn't know. Well, how about if you called thirty of your best friends and neighbors to come help. Do you think you could do it then? What's that you say? It would be a breeze. You could toss that television around like a Caesar salad. Hmm, better not. After all, there's already too much violence on TV...bah-dum-bump!

What's the point of this ridiculous exercise? It's elementary. Some things in life you simply can't do on your own. Lifting a big-screen TV over your head is one of them. Abstinence is another. Sure you can assert yourself, affirm yourself, and love yourself just fine; but you can't achieve abstinence all by yourself. You need help; you need support!

Support is fundamental to the recovery from any addiction. Consider the plight of alcoholics. For years their disease was hidden in a lonely shroud of shame and denial. Alcoholics had no support, and as a result, they seldom found recovery. However, in 1935, Alcoholics Anonymous (AA) was established as a voluntary communion of men and women who support each other in attaining sobriety. Its success has been phenomenal. Currently AA has over 90,000 chapters in 115 countries, helping over 2,000,000 recovering alcoholics learn to live life "one day at a time."

But what about your plight? Is recovery from food addiction any easier? Does it require any less support? Certainly not. In fact, you face an even greater challenge. It's hard enough for an alcoholic to live life one day at a time, but you have to live it one meal at a time, three or four times each day. And while the alcoholic can avoid the temptations inside the tavern or liquor store, you can't avoid your drug. Food is everywhere!

To make matters worse, compulsive overeaters seldom have the unconditional support of their families and friends. Oh sure, if you were a recovering alcoholic they'd rally to your side. Maybe they'd throw out your booze, or at least hide the bottles. But for the recovering overeater, there is no rally cry. Instead you hear a different cry. You hear, "Oh no! You're on another diet. Please God, not another diet." Who can blame them for their skepticism? After all, they've seen plenty of your "miracle" food plans come and go without making a dent in your appetite. "Why should this plan be any different?" they think. It's not that your loved ones don't care about you. They just don't understand the disease.

So what's the solution? Start by asking your family and friends to read this book. You'll be surprised how much support you'll gain once they realize the true nature of your addiction. But don't stop there. Family and friends can carry you only so far. You deserve the best support available. You deserve the support of the thousands who have walked in your shoes and are now walking in recovery. You deserve Overeaters Anonymous (OA).

Like Alcoholics Anonymous, OA is a fellowship of individuals who, through shared experience and mutual support, are finding recovery. There are no dues or fees, nor any affiliations with public or private organizations, political movements, or religious ideologies. The only thing required of you is a sincere desire to stop overeating. For more information, look for OA in the white pages of your phone book. With over 11,000 chapters worldwide, there's bound to be several near you. Don't wait, call today!

Chapter 10

The Menu For Life: Basics

Diet is a Four Letter Word

I made the mistake of asking Ralph, "Hey, how's the diet going?" It seemed like an innocent enough question at the time. But to Ralph, who spent ten years riding the diet yo-yo until finally choosing abstinence, this was an opportunity to teach his scrawny little doctor a thing or two about the real world of dieting. He looked me straight in the eye and made one of the most profound statements I've heard.

"Diets fail," he said. That's it, nothing else–just, "Diets fail." Now I know that doesn't seem like an earth shattering statement, but you don't know Ralph.

Ralph is a kind and peaceful man, but more importantly, he is a powerful man–a six-foot-five, 255 pound, solid muscle man. (I know it's muscle, because he lost over one hundred pounds of fat since discovering abstinence.) Now Ralph is a man of few words; and when a six-foot-five, 255 pound

muscle man of few words speaks–well I don't know about
you, but I listen!

"Diets fail." Such simple wisdom. It's a certainty right
up there with death and taxes. Ninety-eight percent of all
Americans who diet will regain the weight they lose (and
more) within two years. That's a ninety-eight percent failure
rate!

Diets fail for numerous reasons. The majority are restrictive, tasteless, and physically unsound. Fasting, weight
loss shakes, grapefruit, rice diets, and the likes, all neglect
essential nutrients. This leaves your body weak, hungry and
primed for a binge. Many other diets place far too much emphasis on protein. They give you protein powders, protein
shakes, and meat, Meat, MEAT. Not that there's anything
wrong with protein, but too much can damage your liver or
kidneys, and increase your cholesterol. Even worse, diets
known as Very Low Caloric Diets are becoming vogue. These
diets limit you to less than 850 calories per day and yield extremely rapid weight loss; but it's often at the expense of
muscle wasting and fatigue. Strict physician monitoring and
biweekly blood checks are required. For many, dietary com-
pliance is riskier than remaining obese.

Another reason diets fail is that they seldom provide
guidance for maintaining weight loss once you reach your
goal weight. Tabloid and fashion magazines present a new
diet every month. All of them tell you how to lose weight,
but none tell you how to keep it off. The editors realize this.
They know that once you're fat again, you'll toss aside the
old diet and eagerly purchase their next issue in search of
diet Utopia. It's a multi-billion dollar shell game with your
health on the line.

Even more ludicrous is the current trend of joining expensive weight loss centers that actually make you buy
their own brand of food. Their so-called "health foods" are
often loaded with sodium and preservatives. Remember the
old saying "give me a fish and I'll eat for a day, but teach me
to fish and I'll eat for a lifetime." These businesses, and
that's what they are, *businesses*, make money by selling you

the "fish" day after day. Stop it! Unless you're just too busy to prepare your own meals, you'll be far richer, wiser, and healthier following The Menu For Life and "fishing" for yourself.

Besides, even the best diet plans are doomed to fail with compulsive overeaters. Most commercial weight loss centers don't address the relationship between binge food, serotonin, and emotion. Their diets are enormously successful for the rest of the world, but they don't eliminate the foods that can be catastrophic to compulsive overeaters. Sometimes their weight loss bars and shakes contain so many highly processed carbohydrates that they can actually trigger bingeing and make matters worse. I've even seen a few well-known diets actually encourage eating a chocolate bar as a way to curb hunger pains. That's like telling alcoholics to stay on the wagon by having a shot of whiskey whenever they are thirsty. It's utter nonsense.

Why have diets failed you? Too restrictive...too many trigger foods...not enough aftercare? It really doesn't matter. Ultimately, diets fail because they focus on the symptom of your compulsive overeating (weight gain) and neglect your disease. Unless the psychological, social, and biological components of overeating are properly addressed, diets will do only one thing for you–fail!

What's In a Name?

Advertising executives are paid thousands of dollars to sell concept over quality. For example, ask someone to buy a worthless piece of gravel and you would be scorned. But call that same stone a "pet rock" and suddenly you're a millionaire.

Marketers of diets have followed suit by preying upon society's desire for chic rapid cures. Attention grabbing titles like the *Scarsdale,* or *Paris* diets attract consumers on name alone, as if wealth adds credibility to the diet's content. It does not!

For those not easily impressed by glamorous hype, marketers have a backup plan–DECEIT. Who can resist titles like *Thin-So-Fast* or *Fat-To-Muscle Diet*? They're catchy, promising, and oooooh-so misleading. These are the Chia Pets and hula hoops of diets. They are very trendy, but destined to fade without making any significant contributions to weight loss. Compulsive overeaters have been the trendsetters for these transient remedies all too often. It's time for a change.

What separates The Menu For Life from all diets begins with its name. No glamour, glitz, or gimmicks–just a straight forward unpretentious name. Webster's defines *life* as both "a way of living," as well as "the experiences that make up the existence of a person." The Menu For Life has such a dual meaning.

In one respect, The Menu For Life offers a unique way of living–a lifelong pattern of healthful eating. On the other hand, it recognizes that compulsive overeating isn't just about food, but rather a summation of biological, psychological, and sociological experiences. Because of this dual meaning, The Menu For Life offers you this challenge: for every pound of flesh lost, a pound of self-awareness should be gained.

The Menu at a Glance

Too often fad diets, and even supervised programs, focus so narrowly on weight reduction that other body systems are completely ignored. You lose weight, but at what expense–kidney, heart, liver disease, or even death? Thank goodness for The Menu For Life–a serotonin-friendly food plan that offers a wide range of magnificent health benefits. These include:

1. Lower cholesterol levels
2. Decreased blood pressure
3. Improved control of diabetes
4. Improved sleep

5. Reduced symptoms of chronic gastrointestinal disorders including irritable bowel syndrome, constipation, and hemorrhoids
6. Increased energy

These benefits aren't unique or revolutionary. Anyone following RDA guidelines will likely note similar improvements. Unfortunately, the struggle to eat a balanced diet is undermined by compulsive overeating–a disease that constantly seeks to medicate itself with nutritionally empty binge food. Failure to recognize this illness is the shortcoming of most well-respected food plans.

The Menu For Life not only recognizes this disorder, but directly addresses the needs of the compulsive overeater by creating a meal plan that places its emphasis on three key elements:

1. Nutrition
2. Satisfaction
3. Trigger Food Elimination

The Menu For Life is divided into two phases: The Menu For Less, followed by The Menu For A Lifetime. Both phases replace binge food with a balance of high quality protein (the source of tryptophan and serotonin) and whole complex carbohydrates (foods that release insulin evenly, so your serotonin levels can finally stabilize.) The result–no more mood swings! Furthermore, The Menu For Life provides "whole" foods that take more time to digest, so you feel full longer–so no more cravings! And most importantly, The Menu For Life stresses vitamins, minerals, and fiber, *not* calories. You will feel full on fewer calories–so no more bingeing–no more weight gain!

Will you lose weight? Definitely! How does eight to twelve pounds a month sound? That's what The Menu For Less can do for you. Best of all, there's none of that maddening calorie counting to further your obsession with food. Instead, you're provided with an easy-to-follow template that highlights the major food groups for each meal. Your choice of foods are virtually endless and easily measured (i.e., one cup salad, one medium apple). Weight loss no longer has to seem like a full-time job. It can be a year-round vacation!

Once you reach your goal weight, you are ready for The Menu For A Lifetime; a multi-tiered program that progressively builds on the foundation of The Menu For Less. It's innovative design allows you to finally stop the diet yo-yo and keep weight off–for life! So throw away your elastic waistbands, belt hole puncher, and 2XXLs–you won't be needing them any more. Welcome to The Menu For Life.

Chapter 11

Nutrition 101

Food Basics

Food comes in a variety of shapes, sizes, tastes, and textures. Your tongue, like Star Trek's Captain James Kirk, has a tendency to react over-dramatically to the myriad of senstions food produces. The remainder of your body, however, is like Mr. Spock–unemotionally processing food into six basic nutrients: water, carbohydrates, fats, proteins, vitamins, and minerals. An adequate supply of these essentials and your Enterprise is cruising along at warp nine. But neglect one or another, and not even Mr. Scott can get your engines running!

Water

No calories and no taste–it's hard to believe that water is the most important nutrient there is. You can conceivably go weeks without food, but you'd be dead in days without good old fashion H_20. Why? Because water is the sea on which all your life sustaining chemical reactions set sail. It bathes your organs, cools your body, and shuttles nutrients to every cell. Unfortunately, water vanishes from your body faster than a desert mirage. You lose three quarts per day through sweat, urine, feces, and even through the vapor of your breath. As such, The Menu For Life recommends a minimum of sixty-four ounces of water per day. If plain old water is too bland, try jazzing it up with a wedge of lemon or tickling your lips with some bubbly soda water.

Carbohydrates

Just because I haven't said too many kind words about carbohydrates doesn't mean I hate them. Carbohydrates are your most important energy source; they should constitute more than 50% of your daily calories. But beware! All carbohydrates are not created equally.

Nutritionists classify carbohydrates into two groups: **simple** and **complex**. Simple carbohydrates are sugars. It doesn't matter what name they hide behind: sucrose, glucose, fructose, or maltose, a sugar by any other name is still a sugar–simple. On the other hand, complex carbohydrates are quite distinct. They are molecular strands of hundreds or thousands of sugars united together and combined with various nutrients. Given their complexity, it's helpful to subclassify them into **processed** and **whole** carbohydrates.

Processed carbohydrates are grain products that have their bran removed through milling. Removing the bran strips carbohydrates of their fiber, vitamins, and minerals. As a result, their "wholeness" is forever gone. The more carbohydrates are processed, the more unstructured an sugarlike they become. Vital nutrients are lost, leaving only empty calories to wage war on your serotonin system.

Whole carbohydrates retain their bran. So unlike processed carbohydrates, whole carbohydrates aren't warehouses of densely packed calories. Instead, they are your most important sources of fiber, vitamins, and minerals–all of which are *calorie-free*. Yes, calorie-free! That's why a whole jumbo grapefruit, rich in vitamin C, has 25% fewer calories than ten itty-bitty sugary jelly beans. Whole carbohydrates are the main ingredients in The Menu For Life. They include grains, legumes, fruits, and vegetables–a plethora of foods that are all part of an active healthy lifestyle. However, there are a few caveats. Certain exotic fruits like mangos, papaya, or passion fruit, and some starchy vegetables like potatoes and corn are quite high in natural sugars. Since these foods contain vitamins, minerals, and fiber, they're perfectly acceptable. However, their high sugar content can trigger cravings if eaten too often. What's too often? Don't worry, the chapter entitled The Menu For Life Specifics will give you all the details.

Perhaps the most controversial aspect of The Menu For Life is the recommendation to initially abstain from many processed carbohydrates that are considered healthy; foods such as bread and pasta. These foods are healthy for most people; but for compulsive overeaters, these seemingly innocent foods are often triggers for bingeing.

Many of our clients proudly profess their abstinence from cakes, pies, and snack foods, only to sheepishly confess that they still eat a loaf of bread or a pound of spaghetti in one sitting. Sorry noodle lovers, but abstaining from *all* processed carbohydrates while on The Menu For Less is crucial to breaking the addictive cycle and eliminating cravings. Nothing can be gained from bread or pasta that can't be gained from whole grains, fruits, and vegetables–nothing, that is but *pounds*!

Once you reach your goal weight and begin The Menu For A Lifetime, there may be room for an occasional doughy indulgence. But be honest with yourself–better yet, ask your friends and family to help you be brutally honest. If you or your loved ones feel that bread or pasta is one of your binge foods, don't risk relapse. Just continue abstaining, and enjoy the rewards that fruits, vegetables, and whole grains offer. But if you're genuinely convinced that these foods have never been problematic, then feel free to integrate them into The Menu For A Lifetime. If cravings or weight gain return, then you've learned a valuable lesson you shouldn't repeat. But if all goes well...Enjoy!

Fats and Cholesterol

Without question, fat is the most maligned and misunderstood of all nutrients. Store shelves are stocked with countless products claiming their freedom from fat. Other products tout their ability to burn fat and rid its evil presence from your body. Yes it's true, the typical American diet is far too rich in fat. It's also true that the link between excess fat and heart disease is as solid as they come. Nevertheless, there are many woefully tall-tales (or maybe I should say "fat-tales") that need to be clarified.

Tale #1	Fat should be eliminated from my diet.
Fact #1	Even people trying to lose weight should obtain twenty percent of their daily calories from fat.
Tale #2	I should eat only vegetables that are low in cholesterol.
Fact #2	Cholesterol is found solely in animal products. All plants are cholesterol-free.
Tale #3	I greatly reduced cholesterol from my diet, therefore my cholesterol level must be low.
Fact #3	Genetics has far more to with cholesterol levels than does diet. Eighty-five percent of your cholesterol is made by the liver. Only fifteen percent comes from diet. You can eliminate all the cholesterol from your diet and still have an elevated level if your body is making too much on it's own.

With so many myths and misconceptions concerning fat, the necessity of a moderate amount is often overlooked. Of all available nutrients, fat delivers the most concentrated source of calories. For better or for worse, one gram of fat contains over twice as many calories as one gram of either carbohydrate or protein. This makes fat an ideal source of stored energy that supplies fuel to your body in times of need. Fat also protects and cushions your organs as it insulates your body from the cold. More importantly, fat is an integral part of your cells' membranes, nerve sheaths, and sex hormones. A limited amount of fat is vital to your health. In fact, in the medical community, life without fat has a specific name–Death! But which fats are healthy to eat? Is there even such a thing as "healthy fat?" Let's start with cholesterol, the fat you have grown to hate.

Everyone remembers the Wicked Witch of the West in *The Wizard of Oz*. But who recalls Glenda, and Dorthy's paradoxical question, "Are you a good witch or a bad witch?" It may be hard to believe, but when it comes to cholesterol, there are also good and bad witches.

One type of cholesterol, known as low density lipoprotein (or LDL), is a very bad witch. It casts a spell upon your arteries that can harden, thicken, and eventually clog them completely. Thankfully, there is high density lipoprotein (or HDL), the good witch. HDL does its best to reverse LDL's hex by removing excess cholesterol from your arteries; and just for good measure, it helps transport vitamins D, E, A, and K into your bloodstream. Your liver makes plenty of HDL all by itself, so you really don't need to eat any cholesterol at all. But if you're like most Americans, you spray an extra 500 mg of "bad cholesterol" on the walls of your blood vessels each and every day, staining your arteries with a needless excess of cholesterol graffiti.

Next let's look at saturated fat. Why is it called *saturated*? Well, there is a complex chemical reason, but I prefer a much simpler explanation: it saturates your nice clean arteries with ugly, fatty goop. In fact, saturated fat is even more instrumental in increasing your cholesterol level than cholesterol consumption itself. It's a definite artery blocker. Foods high in saturated fat include beef, pork, and lamb, as well as fat from dairy products. Poultry has less saturated fat than beef, and fish has far less than either. Surprisingly, two vegetable oils (coconut and palm) contain the highest relative percentage of saturated fat. In times when most vegetable oils are rightfully encouraged over animal fats, be on the lookout for these two oils. Some companies mislead consumers by boasting that their product is made with vegetable oil. Unfortunately, they are often using the less healthy palm or coconut oil.

You've seen fat's bad side, now let's take a look at the good. Meet Mono- and Polyunsaturated–the Batman and Robin of fat. This Dynamic Duo lowers cholesterol levels and minimizes LDL's sinister doings within your arteries. Look for polyunsaturated fats in vegetable oils derived from corn, safflower, soybean, sunflower, and cottonseed. But don't stop looking there. It's the mono-unsaturated fats that seem to be the most beneficial of the pair. You can find them in certain nuts, avocados, or olives. Isn't it nice to know there's a fat or two you don't have to hate?

The Menu For Life acknowledges the good, the bad, and the ugly in fat. It keeps saturated fat and cholesterol to a minimum by having you cut meats lean and recommending poultry or fish over red meat. It says, "No thank you" to palm, coconut, or animal oils, and opts for the zesty flavor of several healthier oils (olive, safflower, etc.).

Lastly, whether it's a good witch or a bad witch, fat is still a witch–a calorie heavy witch! That's why The Menu For Life limits fat to a sparse but healthy amount, creating not a fat-free diet, but hopefully a fat-free you.

Protein

You're on the *Family Feud*. Richard Dawson tells you that one hundred people were asked to name a nutrient. What was the number one response? Survey says–Protein!

When most people think of nourishment, they think of protein, and for good reason. With the exception of water, protein is the most common substance in the body. Protein provides the building blocks for your skin, muscles, cartilage, and organs. Protein enzymes speed up your body's chemical reactions, and protein antibodies fight off infection. Several hormones, including insulin, are protein-based. Even hemoglobin, the stuff in your blood that carries oxygen, is a protein.

Your body can't make good use of dietary protein until it is first broken down into smaller components called *amino acids*. These are the Leggos of the body. They come in a limited variety of shapes and sizes, but the combinations they form are limitless. Humans require twenty different amino acids in order to make all the protein your body demands. Your liver manufactures eleven of them, but the remaining nine must be obtained from food. These nine are known as *essential* amino acids.

Foods that contain all nine essential amino acids are called *complete* proteins. With the exception of gelatin, all animal proteins, like beef, chicken, fish, and pork are complete. Believe it or not, egg whites are the most concentrated package of essential amino acids available. They are almost pure protein. But nature doesn't force us to be carnivores to get the essential amino acids we need. There is room for vegetarians as well.

Vegetarians obtain essential amino acids in two ways. Option one is tofu. Soybean is a great quality complete protein, containing all nine essentials. But day after day of tofu steaks, tofu soup, tofu pudding, tofu...Tofu...TOFU can grow boring, so most vegetarians go for option two: *complimentary incomplete* proteins.

The majority of vegetable proteins are incomplete, meaning they lack one or more essential amino acids. But by eating—oh let's say rutabaga (which lacks amino acid B, but has plenty of amino acid A) with kumquats (which have B, but no A), a complete protein is created. Most nations have discovered ways to create their own culturally acceptable complete protein combination. In India it is lentils and rice. In the Middle East it's the mix of chic peas and sesame that forms humus. In the United States we use peanut butter and bread–and if you know anyone who combines rutabaga and kumquats on a regular basis–run! They've gotta be from Mars.

Whether it's tofu, T-bones, or even rutabaga you prefer, The Menu For Life delivers the right amount of high quality protein–enough to keep your muscles firm and strong as you lose weight, but not anywhere near the protein overdose so many fad diets encourage. Remember, protein is only a soldier in the "battle of the bulge." Whole complex carbohydrates are the generals.

Vitamins

Vitamins are micronutrients–they are the body's spice. Have you ever made a recipe that called for a pinch of oregano or a dash of paprika, only to discover that you didn't have the ingredient? Well, if you chose to ignore the ingredient, chances are you noticed a difference. The dish just wasn't up to par. Vitamins are like that. They have no calories, and your body requires "just a sprinkle," but neglect one or more and you won't feel up to par either.

Lucky #13. That's how many different vitamins you require to maintain growth and development. These can be divided into two groups: those that dissolve in fat (vitamins D, E, A and K) and those that dissolve in water (vitamins C and the eight B complex vitamins). Somehow, your body must sense how crucial vitamins are, because it can stockpile these nutritional acorns in large enough quantities to last for weeks.

The "RDA" (Recommended Daily Allowance) gives a rough estimate of the amount of vitamins the average person needs to prevent deficiencies and stay healthy. It's a teeny-tiny amount (something the majority of Americans can easily obtain by eating a well-balanced diet). In fact, according to most nutritionists, you really have to follow a relatively bizarre diet to develop any vitamin deficiencies. So then, why is half of America spending their hard earned money on vitamin pills they don't need? Who knows. Some tell me that it's holistic medicine. "Okay," I say, "but what is more holistic; getting your vitamins from whole grain cereals, fruits, and vegetables, or popping a mass produced, artificially colored, flavored, and sweetened dinosaur-shaped supplement?" Anyone? Anyone?

While we are on the subject, vitamins are called micronutrients for good reason. *Only small amounts are needed!* In fact, if you take too many vitamins, they can act as free floating drugs instead of nutrients. Like all drugs, vitamins have the potential for side effects and can be lethal. Of course this doesn't stop vitamin hucksters from pawning off their candy-coated surplus on you. And that's not all. They are also willing to pummel your body with potentially deadly rocks. Rocks otherwise known as...

...Minerals

The human body is a chemical blend of less than forty elements. Four of these: carbon, oxygen, hydrogen and nitrogen, are the backbone of all nutrients. Together they account for 96% of your body weight. The thirty-plus elements that make up the rest of you are called minerals. Seven major minerals: calcium, phosphorus, sulfur, potassium, sodium, chloride and magnesium, constitute the overwhelming majority of your total mineral weight. The remainder are known as trace minerals. They include: iron, zinc, copper, iodine and fluorine.

Minerals are the Napoleons of the nutrient world. They are small in stature, but still powerful leaders. Minerals regulate such central processes as heart beat, nerve conduction, and fluid balance. They transport oxygen to your cells and haul waste products away. They even give your bones stability—so you aren't as limp as a rubber chicken.

As with vitamins, a balanced diet provides most people with all the minerals required for health. Of course that's not what advertisers want you to believe. They have convinced us that without extra calcium, iron, or their mineral *de jour*, the world would be full of brittle boned, anemic invalids. Not true! In fact, 10% of the population absorbs too many minerals. For this substantial minority, long-term supplementation can lead to mineral overload, and even death.

So that settles it then—no vitamin pills for you. Wrong! Compulsive overeaters need a daily multivitamin/mineral supplement while on The Menu For Less. You see, most compulsive overeaters do follow a rather "bizarre" diet–a diet high in HPCs, sugar, and fat–a diet plundered of vitamins and minerals. In view of this, compulsive overeaters are prone to subtle nutritional deficiencies and require initial supplementation. Additionally, The Menu For Less provides far fewer than 2000 calories per day. Most nutritionists agree that if your daily intake is under 2000 calories, a multivitamin/mineral supplement is beneficial.

The supplement you chose should be sugar-free and contain no more than 150% of any RDA recommendation. Centrum and Therogram are good choices. Once you begin The Menu For A Lifetime, supplements should no longer be necessary. You'll be eating such a wide variety of foods in enough quantity that you won't have any trouble getting what you need–100% holistic, all natural, vitamins and minerals.

You Are What You Eat

Ralph describes his binge eating days like this:

They were as empty and disappointing as the nutritionally void foods I once craved. But now that I'm on The Menu For Life, I feel completely enriched. My life is whole, and the world isn't passing me by any more. I'm finally fulfilled.

How fulfilled are you? Is your life gratifying, or is it as discouraging as your last binge? Change may be just a meal away. The Menu For Life: *whole* carbohydrates, *lean* protein, *low fat*, vitamins, and minerals that *satisfy* your needs. "You are what you eat." Hmmm, maybe there's more truth to this than meets the eye.

Chapter 12

Satisfaction

Grrrrrrrr...

From the deepest, darkest recesses, it lays in wait. No man can escape its savagery. Neither beast nor demon can rival its sublime destruction. What is this monestrous creation? It is the Stomach Grumble!

A growling stomach and incessant hunger pains have done more to sabotage your weight loss efforts than any other factor. If you don't feel full, it is hard to focus on anything but your next meal. Satiety (or feeling full) is a prerequisite for successful weight loss.

Compulsive overeaters search in vain for satiety, and at times their quest turns grisly. Take Frank, for example. He tried every diet he could find, but nothing ever satisfied him. Hunger and weight gain always ensued. To Frank, stomach stapling seemed like his only hope. The concept seemed logical—make the stomach smaller and create the feeling of fullness with less food. Well, this may work for some, but certainly not for Frank. He wasn't able to break his emotional attachment to food. Frank, like many other compulsive overeaters who failed this disfiguring surgical procedure, simply ate twice as often and grew more obese. Others have chosen less invasive but equally dangerous ways to achieve satiety. Denise tried the gastric balloon. Under medical supervision she swallowed a small balloon, which was then inflated in order to reduce her stomach's volume. Unfortunately, things didn't go as planned. Denise's balloon accidently dislodged and obstructed her bowels. Emergency surgery saved her life but left her with chronic diarrhea. Others haven't been so lucky. Complications from the gastric balloon have resulted in several deaths.

Thankfully, such barbaric efforts to quiet the Stomach Grumble have fallen into disfavor. Today, attempts at producing satiety focus more on dietary changes, but these too have their dangers. The latest fad diets reduce carbohydrate intake to less than 40 grams a day. This forces the body to choose either fat or protein as its main source of energy. In an effort to prevent muscle loss, the body selectively breaks down fat and produces a fuel known as *ketone*. As the breakdown of fat continues, ketone levels rise, creating an abnormal condition called *ketosis*.

Proponents claim ketosis reduces hunger and liberates fat from the body. I suppose in some respects ketosis does "burn" fat. But where there's smoke there's fire, and ketones are a toxic flame. Ketosis is associated with headaches, nausea, dizziness, malaise, bad breath, potassium deficiency, increased cholesterol, and cardiac arrhythmias. These side effects are so debilitating that most physicians strongly discourage this approach to dieting.

The Satisfaction Solution

If satiety can evade staplings, balloons, and even ketosis, then what's left? The Menu For Life. It takes the only sensible approach toward satiety: fill up on nutrients, not empty calories. Try this next exercise and you'll know exactly what I mean.

Picture twenty-two M&Ms having a party in your belly. Go ahead, picture your favorite ones: the browns, the greens, or maybe the new "cool" blues. Got the image? They fit pretty comfortably, don't they? Lots of room to sing, dance, or argue the politics of "plain" versus "peanut."

Next, picture another belly party with a different guest list. This time you invite one nicely polished bright red apple, a piping hot baked potato, one piece of oven-roasted chicken breast, a cup of fresh green beans, and an ice cold glass of skim milk. Now things seem a little crowded. The potato is getting mashed, the apple is getting bruised, and everybody is crying over the spilled milk. The stomach is filled to capacity.

Why the silly imagery? After all, it doesn't take a physicist to recognize that a sensible meal occupies more space than twenty-two measly M&Ms. But what most of us don't realize is that one melt-in-your-mouth-and-leave-you-craving handful of confection has just as many calories as a modest meal.

Fill the stomach and it will feel full—simple enough. But fill it with nutrients, *not* chocolate coated calories, HPCs, sugar, and fat. Fill it with The Menu For Life: whole grains, fresh fruits, vegetables, and lean meats—foods packed with vitamins, minerals, and fiber, not pounds—foods that are whole, so they take longer to digest—foods that won't cause serotonin to soar—foods that *satisfy*.

Chapter 13

Trigger Foods

Mr. Yuck Saved My Life

When I was just a tike, maybe three-or-four years old, I tasted things. Chalk, ants, mud, you name it, I tasted it. At first my parents didn't mind too much (other than the occasional embarrassment I caused when I licked my neighbor's aluminum siding). But the day I tasted Comet, that kitchen cleansing wonder–which by the way, doesn't taste a thing like a lime Pixie Stix–Mom and Dad's embarrassment turned into fear. Needless to say, Comet didn't kill me, but I did turn a nice ashen color before spewing forth my lunch on our nice Berber carpet. Off to the pediatrician I went.

"Enough is enough," the doctor said, "If you want your boy to live to his next birthday, then bring home Mr. Yuck."

Mr. Yuck was a scowling green-faced decal distributed by the poison control center. Parents stuck Mr. Yuck's ugly mug on all of their household poisons. His message was clear and simple: Do not eat, do not drink, or you will be sick! From that day on, Mr. Yuck lived among us. He was under the kitchen sink, in the medicine cabinet, and in the dirtiest corners of our garage. He was everywhere. I'm pretty sure he saved my life.

Too bad Mr. Yuck isn't stuck to all your binge food. He could point out every food that's toxic to your serotonin system. Avoid these foods, and recovery would be a snap. But sadly, Mr. Yuck is not available. Instead, binge food comes wrapped with wonderfully enticing logos–cuddly Teddy Grahams, friendly Keebler Elves, and a cute little bird that goes, "Cuckoo," for Coco Puffs. How can you possibly avoid binge food when most of it seems so irresistibly innocent?

"Ideal" Abstinence in the "Real" World

In an ideal world life would be perfect. There would be no crime, no poverty, and only fresh, wholesome, natural foods. Sorry, but welcome to the real world–a world with more than its fair share of felons, paupers, and binge foods! And in this real world, "ideal" abstinence is a lofty goal.

Ideal abstinence eliminates all HPCs, sugar, and excess fat...completely. That's right, *completely*! Who has the time to create a food plan like that? I doubt that you do. After all, that's a pretty tall order in a world so thoroughly saturated with junk food. That's why The Menu For Life exists. It does the work for you and makes ideal abstinence hassle-free. But what about the times when The Menu For Life isn't at your fingertips: like dinner parties, company picnics, or a night on the town. What do you do then? Do you spend hours weighing the risks and benefits of every ingredient in the soup du jour? Do you feel like a failure if a grain of sugar slips past your guard? Do you develop a maddening preoccupation with every bite you take? NO, NO, and NO! You've been there and done that. That's the last thing you need! Sometimes, "ideal" abstinence requires some real world modifications–some "real" abstinence.

Real abstinence is a personalized plan against overeating. It's your insurance policy when The Menu For Life just isn't practical. How does it work? Well, remember the Lay's Potato Chip slogan, "Betcha can't eat just one?" Real abstinence recognizes that day after day you take this challenge and lose. Of course it doesn't have to be potato chips. Maybe it's just one specific candy. Maybe it's all pasta. Or maybe it's anything that contains sugar. The point is, there are certain foods you simply can't resist. They feed your feelings so powerfully that they inevitably provoke an enormous binge. These are your *trigger foods*. These are the focus of real abstinence.

Make a list of your trigger foods. Think hard. They are different for everyone. Ask your loved ones to help you. They may be able to point out problem foods you overlooked. Once your list is complete, focus your energy on total abstinence from these foods. If another food or ingredient comes along that triggers cravings or a binge, don't beat yourself up with guilt and negativity. Just add it to your list and avoid it. Before long, you will achieve *real* abstinence in a way that's *ideal* for you.

Let's review your list. How many of your trigger foods contain highly processed carbohydrates? How many contain sugar? How many contain excess fat? How many contain all three??? My guess is almost all. The ones that don't, probably include one of these hidden triggers: sugar aliases, alcohol, or crude-mood-foods. Let's take a closer look at each of these hidden triggers.

Sugar Stage Names

Archibald Leach, Marion Morrison, Norma Jean Baker—who are these people? You probably know them better as Cary Grant, John Wayne, and Marilyn Monroe. Why did they change their names? There's just one logical explanation. Nobody liked their real ones. I mean would you swoon over somebody named Archibald, or call the toughest man ever to grace the silver screen, "Marion?" I think not! When it comes to big-time acting, the right name makes a world of difference.

In the world of compulsive overeating, there's no greater performer than sugar. It plays the role of friend, confidant, and lover, to Academy Award winning perfection. But it's all just an act. The real sugar is nothing more than a two-faced phony–America's number one trigger food! Fortunately, sugar has finally been exposed as the impostor that it is. Stores everywhere are blackballing it and tarnishing its name in a nationwide "sugar-free" campaign. But has this stopped sugar's career? Nope, because sugar is disguised.

Nowadays, sugar goes by several aliases. Look at your list of trigger foods again. Are there ones that don't seem to contain HPCs, sugar, or excess fat, yet you crave them anyway? Check out their ingredients and see if maybe sugar is disguising itself under one of these stage names:

Beet Sugar	Lactose
Brown Sugar	Malto-dextrin
Cane Sugar	Mannitol
Corn Syrup	Maple Sugar
Dextrose	Molasses
Fructose	Rice Sugar
Galactose	Sorbitol
Glucose	Sucrose
Honey	Turbinado Sugar

Don't let these aliases fool you. Sugar by any other name is still sugar; and if it's one of your trigger foods–don't complain, just abstain!

The "Boos" on Booze

"Oh beautiful for spacious skies and amber waves of grain." Imagine rows of wheat, corn, and barley–entire fields of complex carbohydrates swaying rhythmically to a gentle autumn breeze. A picturesque scene, isn't it? But what happens to those amber waves at harvest time? Some are taken by farmers to nourish their families and sustain their livestock. Some are sold at supermarkets or roadside stands to feed the masses. But others are transformed into the ultimate HPC–liquid carbohydrate with a kick–booze! Whether it's beer from barely, wine from grapes, whiskey from rye, or even gin from juniper berries, all complex carbohydrates can be processed, fermented, aged, and distilled into the most powerful sugar known to man–alcohol. Alcoholism runs rampant among compulsive overeaters and their families. Why? Because there's no quicker way to drown your sorrows, toast your successes, or just plain feed your feelings than with alcohol. It's a mind numbing, serotonin surging, nutritionally empty trigger food. Is it on your list? Should it be? If so, just say "No!"

Crunchers, Munchers & Smoothies

Forget all the technical mumbo jumbo for a moment and look at a basic fact. Compulsive overeaters feed feelings. Is it always by way of serotonin? Absolutely not! Sometimes bingeing bypasses biology altogether and pacifies emotions directly through the crude-mood-foods. "What are crude-mood-foods?" you ask. They are the crunchers, munchers, and smoothies–that's any food (processed or whole) that has the right texture, the right size, or even the right sound to instantly feed your feelings.

Have you ever been *angry* and unleashed your aggression with a power-packed CRUNCH from a crisp chip? Have you ever been *bored* enough to pass the idle time with munch after munch of bite-sized peanuts, sunflower seeds, or grapes? Have you ever felt so *lonely* that you nurtured yourself with the smooth, soothing texture of peanut butter, yogurt, or ice cream? If so, then you know exactly what I mean. Maybe you didn't binge on an HPC, sugar, or excess fat, but you binged nevertheless, didn't you? You fed your feelings, and crude-mood-foods were your trigger.

How many crude-mood-foods are on your list of triggers? How many should be? Remember, abstinence isn't just about avoiding foods that manipulate serotonin. It's about living in the here and now, and expressing your feelings, not feeding them. So whether it's HPCs, sugar, and excess fat, or crunchers, munchers, and smoothies–if it feeds your mood, avoid the food!

On Your Mark, Get Set, GOAL

You are oh-so close to starting The Menu For Life. But there's one thing left to do–select your goal weight. Why? For one simple reason. Compulsive overeaters who reach their goal are far more likely to keep weight off than those who merely come close. Here's how to determine your own personal goal weight.

Wrap the thumb and index finger of your right hand around your left wrist. If your thumb and index finger overlap, you are small framed. If they just meet, then you are medium framed. If instead they don't even touch, then you are large framed. Now turn to the Appendix and locate your height. Compare your height to your frame and behold, your ideal weight. Of course by now you know this isn't an ideal world, so what's the point of an ideal weight? A *realistic* weight makes a lot more sense. So determine your ideal weight and then set your goal weight within 5% of that number. Now you are really ready to "go for the goal" and put compulsive overeating behind you.

Chapter 14

The Menu For Life: Specifics

Freedom From Food Addiction

Breaking free from an addictive cycle is never easy. This is especially true for compulsive overeaters. It's nearly impossible to recognize and eliminate all the foods that feed your feelings. Fortunately, The Menu For Life does most of this work for you. It replaces trigger foods with quality protein and whole complex carbohydrates that enable you to feel full, create energy, and burn unwanted calories. Before you know it, you truly will be the "fairest of them all."

As discussed previously, The Menu For Life is divided into two phases: The Menu For Less and The Menu For A Lifetime. The first phase (The Menu For Less) stabilizes serotonin, eliminates cravings, and allows you to reach your goal weight. Then it's time for The Menu For A Lifetime. This multi-phase program provides you with the additional nutrients necessary to maintain and stabilize your weight throughout your entire binge-free life.

The Menu For Less

	Breakfast	Lunch	Dinner	Metabolic (bed time)
Dairy	1 cup			1 cup
Cereal	Females 1/2 cup* Males 1 cup			1/2 cup*
Starch		Females 1/2 cup Males 1 cup	1 cup	
Salad		1 cup	1 cup	
Vegetable		1 cup fresh or 1/2 cup cooked	1 cup fresh or 1/2 cup cooked	
Fruit	1 piece fresh* or 1 cup fresh/frozen or 1/2 cup canned	1 piece fresh* or 1 cup fresh/frozen or 1/2 cup canned		1 piece fresh* or 1 cup fresh/frozen or 1/2 cup canned
Protein		3 oz	Females 3 oz Males 4 oz	
Fat		1 tsp*	1 tsp*	

* unless otherwise directed

Dairy   1 cup Skim Milk

1 cup Yogurt (low-fat/sugar-free)

Cereal   1/2 cup* of any cereal that has sugar listed as fourth or lower ingredient. Examples include:

Oat or Wheat Bran	Oatmeal
Cream of Rye or Wheat®	Nutrigrain®
Grainfields Cereal®	Uncle Sams®
Shredded Wheat®	

1-1/2 cup of any puffed cereal
1/4 cup of Granola or Grape Nuts®

* males should double the cereal serving size for breakfast

Starch   Lunch: 1/2 cup for females/1 cup for males
Dinner: 1 cup for females and males

Barley	Yams
Brown/Wild/Long-grain Rice	Succotash
Corn	Squash
Garbanzo or Navy Beans	Peas
Kashi	Lima beans
Kidney or Chili Beans	
Potato - medium sized	

Salad   1 cup

Salads should contain at least 3 different vegetables (see listing on next page). It's best to eat one cup of hot vegetable and one cup of salad at both lunch and dinner. You can, however, substitute 2 cups of salad or 2 cups of hot vegetable in place of one or the other.

Vegetables 1 cup fresh/1/2 cup cooked
Select from the following:

Asparagus	Mushrooms
Alfalfa Sprouts	Okra
Artichokes	Onions
Beans: Green or Yellow	Parsley
Bean Sprouts	Peppers
Beets	Pickles (dill only)
Broccoli	Radishes
Brussel Sprouts	Rutabaga
Cabbage	Sauerkraut
Carrots	Snow Peas
Cauliflower	Spinach
Celery	Tomatoes
Collard Greens	Turnip
Cucumbers	Turnip Greens
Eggplant	Water Chestnuts
Kale	Lettuce

Fruit 1 small to medium piece/1/2 cup fresh, frozen, or canned (unless otherwise specified)

Apple	* Kiwi
Applesauce - 1/2 cup	* Mango - 1/2 small
Apricots - 3 medium	Nectarine
Banana	Orange
Blackberries - 3/4 cup	* Papaya - 1 cup
Blueberries - 3/4 cup	Peach
Boysenberries - 3/4 cup	Pear
Cantaloupe - 1/3 medium	Pineapple - 1/2 cup
* Cherries - 12	Plums - 2 small
Cranberries - 1 cup	Pomegranate - 1/2 large
* Grapes - 12 medium	Prunes - 4 small
Grapefruit - 1/2 large	Strawberries 1-1/4 cup
Honeydew - 1/8 medium	Tangerines - 2 small
	* Watermelon - 1 cup

* Denotes fruits that may be associated with cravings and/or bingeing in some compulsive overeaters. Use them sparingly.

Protein   Lunch: 3 oz
Dinner: 3 oz for females, 4 oz for males

Cook protein before weighing. All meats should be cut lean. Remove all visible fat. You may cook chicken with the skin on, but remove it before eating. Keep bacon, sausage, ribs, hot dogs and regular cheeses to a minimum as they are too high in fat. Select from the following:

Fish	Egg Whites (4)
Chicken	Soy Protein
Turkey	Legumes
Veal	Feta/Mozzarella/
Pork	Fat-Free Cheese
Lamb	Cottage/ Ricotta
Beef	Cheese-3/4 cup
Duck	

Fats   1 teaspoon regular/1 tablespoon low fat

Butter	Olive Oil
Mayonnaise	Corn Oil
Margarine	Safflower Oil
Tartar Sauce	Canola Oil
Salad Dressing	

Sour Cream (2 tbsp. regular/3 tbsp. low-fat)

Beverages   **Eight - 8 oz.** glasses of water per day

<u>Optional</u>

• Coffee or tea (sugar-free/no more than 2 cups daily)
• Soda (sugar-free/no more than 2 per day)
• Plain or sugar-free seltzer

Condiments Optional

- Equal or Sweet-n-low (6 per day)
- Lemon wedges (2 per meal)
- Cinnamon (1 teaspoon per meal)
- Chewing gum (sugar-free/6 per day)
- Sauces (1/2 cup per meal includes: ketchup, salsa, etc.)
- All spices (1 tablespoon per meal)
- Horseradish (1 tablespoon per meal)
- Mustard (1 tablespoon per meal)
- Steak Sauce (1 tablespoon per meal)
- Tomato Sauce (1 tablespoon per meal)
- Vinegar (1 tablespoon per meal)

MENU FOR A LIFETIME

The Menu For A Lifetime is designed for compulsive overeaters who are at or below their target weight, or are losing weight too rapidly on the Menu For Less. Remain in Phase 1 for a minimum of two weeks. If after two weeks you've lost four or more pounds, then go to the next phase and repeat the process. If on the other hand you've gained more than four pounds, then return to the previous phase. Once you've found a phase where weight stabilization occurs, remain in that phase, weighing yourself every two weeks and adjusting the phases accordingly. Use the Menu For Less as your guide and augment as follows:

Phase 1   Add one fruit to any meal.

Phase 2   Add one starch to any meal. Include whole grain bread (1 slice) or whole grain pasta (1 cup) if not considered a trigger food.

Phase 3   Add one serving vegetable to any meal.

Phase 4   Add one serving protein to any meal.

Abstinent Guidelines

1. All food should be weighed and measured. You can buy a food scale at most retail stores for just a few dollars.

2. Sit down for your meals without aggravation or confrontation. Eat slowly and gently. Enjoy your food.

3. Don't skip meals. Follow The Menu For Life at breakfast, lunch, dinner, and bedtime to keep your metabolism at peak performance.

4. Do not modify the amount of food recommended by The Menu For Life. At times it may seem like you're eating too much, but the amount specified is necessary for you to feel satisfied throughout the day.

5. Weigh yourself only once every two weeks. Don't obsess. You will lose weight!

6. Variety is the spice of life. Keep The Menu For Life exciting. Don't bore yourself by using the same foods over and over again.

7. Plan ahead. Think of The Menu For Life as your American Express Card—Don't leave home without it.

8. Check with your doctor before starting this or any other food plan.

9. Take a sugar-free multivitamin daily when on The Menu For Less.

10. If certain abstinent foods trigger cravings, eliminate them from The Menu For Life.

11. When in doubt, leave it out. Avoid HPCs, sugar, and excess fat.

The FAQs of Life: Frequently Asked Questions about The Menu For Life

Question: I've been abstinent for close to six months, and I'm almost at my goal weight. My family wants me to take a day off from The Menu For Life. Is this okay?

Answer: That's probably not a good idea. Remember, compulsive overeating is not only an emotional and spiritual disease, it's a physical disease as well. Your body reacts differently to sugar and HPCs. Once your serotonin roller coaster starts to move, it becomes nearly impossible to stop. Your body will begin to insist that you feed it more, and more, and more. After all, if it was as simple as being able to splurge one day, then get back on the wagon the next, you never would have picked up this book.

Question: I've been abstinent for a year, and I think I know how much to eat. Do I still need to weigh and measure my food?

Answer: Absolutely. Compulsive overeaters eat according to emotions, not physical needs. Some days you may know how much is appropriate, but what about the days you're feeling angry, lonely, or sad? When you feed your feelings, your eyes lie and your stomach denies, but cups and scales speak the truth. Stick to weighing and measuring.

Question: What do I do if I forget to eat my fruit at lunch?

Answer: That depends. If you remember at 2, 3, or 4 in the afternoon and you're hungry, then go ahead and eat it. However, if you remember at dinner time, just go ahead and eat your normal dinner and don't add the forgotten fruit.

Question: I don't like breakfast. Why is this meal so important?

Answer: The Menu For Life was designed to satisfy your needs, not your wants. Your body *needs* nourishment in the morning to keep your metabolism at peak efficiency. Also, a hearty breakfast will eliminate any pre-lunch cravings. So give your body what it needs. Give it breakfast each and every morning.

Question: I can't imagine living without sugar or HPCs for the rest of my life. I don't even think it's possible. Help!

Answer: This program is designed to be taken one day at a time. I imagine that thinking about a lifetime of anything feels overwhelming, but all you have to do is stay abstinent today. Can you live without eating sugar for today only? The answer is, yes. You can be abstinent one day at a time.

Question: What if I don't want to follow The Menu For Life? Can I create my own food plan?

Answer: Well, my guess is that you have already tried several of your own and none of them worked. The Menu For Life is different. It is tailor-made for compulsive overeaters. So instead of wasting time trying diet after diet, put your energy into your spiritual and emotional recovery where it belongs, and stick with The Menu For Life.

Question: I've been on The Menu For Life for three days. I'm getting headaches and feeling tired. What's happening?

Answer: It's called detox. Your body is suffering from sugar withdrawal. Common symptoms include headache, fatigue, and irritability. Don't worry, they'll be gone in a few days, after your body cleanses itself from sugary toxins. Soon you'll be feeling better than you have in years.

Question: Why do I have to eat at bedtime, and does it matter what time of the day I eat?

Answer: Your body begins to metabolize food as soon as it is eaten. Each food type is metabolized at different rates, with fat taking the longest to metabolize (approximately five hours). The time of day you chose to eat is not nearly as important as eating your meals four-to-five hours apart (in order to avoid cravings). If you skip your nighttime metabolic meal, you will go 10 hours or more without nourishment. This leaves your metabolism sluggish and your body primed for a binge.

Question: Since I started The Menu For Life I haven't had any cravings, but I still find myself obsessing about what to eat each day. Is there anything I can do to stop this?

Answer: Try this. Every night, before you go to bed, write down your menu for the following day. List each meal, the amounts, and the types of food you intend to eat. Here's an example:

Breakfast

1/2 cup shredded wheat
1 cup skim milk
1 cup strawberries

Lunch

3 oz turkey
1/2 cup brown rice
1 cup fresh green beans
1 cup salad
1 tsp. salad dressing
1 apple

Dinner

3 oz roast beef
1 medium baked potato
1 cup fresh broccoli
1 cup salad
1 tsp. salad dressing

Metabolic

1 cup skim milk
1/2 cup puffed rice
1 orange

This type of pre-planning will help alleviate your obsession. It's important to keep this daily menu in a consistent and central location, like on the refrigerator door or in your wallet. Refer to it whenever your mind starts to drift toward thoughts of food. Having your menu planned and ready will let you focus on life—not on your next meal.

Question: Sometimes I don't feel like eating an entire meal. Do I have to eat all the food allotted?

Answer: Many times during recovery, emotions will interfere with your desire to eat. But don't forget that adding or subtracting food, based on how you feel, got you into this mess. Follow The Menu For Life consistently. It will give you the balanced wholesome food your body needs to stay healthy, clean, and sober.

Question: What can I do to increase my chances of staying committed to abstinence?

Answer: Clean it up. No, I don't mean clean up the dishes. Be emotionally clean with your food. Compulsive overeaters are shame-based perfectionists. You expect your abstinence to be perfect, and when it's not, the shame you feel provides the perfect excuse to binge. Well let's get one thing straight. No one has or ever will attain perfect abstinence. If that's your goal, you're bound to fail. Now that's not a reason to abandon abstinence or not follow The Menu For Life to the best of your ability. It's just reality.

"Clean it up" means finding a supportive friend and letting him/her know exactly what you did with your food. Did you eat what you said you would? Did you weigh and measure all your food? Did you eat it all? If not–tell on yourself!

Okay, go ahead and laugh. I know this sounds silly, but being left to your own devices doesn't work. Compulsive overeaters don't make good choices about food. "Cleaning it up" improves your choices. It keeps you honest, keeps you abstinent, and keeps you sane.

Question: What harm can one little cookie do every now and then?

Answer: Plenty! The obvious answer is that compulsive overeaters can't reliably stop at just one cookie. One is too much and twenty isn't enough. More importantly, one little 50-calorie cookie can really foil all of your efforts to lose weight. In fact, if you ate just one extra cookie each day, you would likely gain an additional five pounds per year. Now, imagine the result if you couldn't stop at just one!

Question: Will I lose weight every week that I'm on The Menu For Less?

Answer: Not necessarily. In fact, many of our clients report losing *inches* around their waist and hips before they notice a discernible loss in weight. Also, keep in mind that your body is in a constant state of change. Whether you are male or female, there are certain times when your body retains fluid. During these times, your weight may fluctuate by several pounds. So don't let the number on the scale make or break your day. Just keep reminding yourself that you are on the best darn food plan available to compulsive overeaters. You *will* lose weight!

Chapter 15

Fit or Fat

"Eat Less, Exercise More!"

How many times have you heard this mystical solution for weight loss—ten, twenty, one thousand times? It's the mantra of every thin person you know. Bob, from the shop says, "Hey, it looks like you could stand to lose a few pounds, why don't you eat less and exercise more." Aunt Betty Boop corners you at the family reunion, "Darling," she says, "I'm worried about your figure. You really should eat less and exercise more." Even your own doctor, the one person you thought understood your compulsion, just stares at you with a look of concern and then spits out the same senseless blather, "I know you're not feeling well, but the best advice I can give you is...EAT LESS, EXERCISE MORE."

Gee, thanks for the swell advice.

How on earth did you ever survive without their uncanny wisdom? Eat less, exercise more. It's so simple now, isn't it?

Well, here's a few questions for those Mr./Ms. Know-it-alls in your life.

What if you have a disease that compels you to eat?

What do you do if you can't eat less?

What if your body is so polluted with sugar that you don't have one ounce of energy to use on exercise?

What then? What? WHAT? **WHAT?**

My guess is that if you ever asked those smarty-pants know-it-alls any of these questions, you would find dead air silence as their response. They can't possibly answer what they do not understand; and believe me, they don't have a clue about compulsive overeating.

You know darn well that you've tried, and tried, and tried again to eat less and exercise more. It didn't work. What's worse, the whole thing got reversed. You ate more and exercised less. You couldn't help it. You are a binge food addict, and nothing Aunt Betty Boop says will change that.

"Eat less, exercise more." It's been a futile proposition, an obstacle you couldn't possibly overcome, until now—until The Menu For Life.

Exercise and The Menu For Life

Talk about a match made in heaven. Exercise and The Menu For Life are your own personal body guards in the battle against compulsive overeating. See how they land the one-two punch on your arch enemies: Weight Gain and Cravings.

Weight Gain: There's no doubt you'll lose weight on The Menu For Life. Exercise will hasten the process, making certain that it's fat you are losing, and not lean muscle.

Cravings: The Menu For Life abolishes cravings by eliminating your trigger foods. Exercise helps seal the deal. A vigorous workout actually increases serotonin. Research suggests that daily exercise lifts serotonin levels as much as fifty percent. Now that's an exercise bonus you can definitely use.

"Eat less, exercise more." This impossible dream can finally be realized. There's only one thing left to do...

...Shape Up!

You did it. You hated it. You did it again, and hated it even more. Now, you just avoid it. EXERCISE! The only "four-letter" word that's eight letters long. Maybe you aren't aware of this, but the word *exercise* is Latin for "please God, make the agony stop." Okay, so maybe it's not. But why do my clients look so tortured when I mention exercise? I mean they squirm, babble incoherent excuses, roll their eyes, and make rude faces? Geez, if they weren't so out of shape, they probably would jump from their chairs and run right out the door.

Can getting in shape really be all that bad? Of course not. It's only as bad as *you* make it. So why have you made exercise seem so bad? Well, I have my theory. Yes! My very own theory. It's called The Great Exercise Myth, and you have fallen victim to it.

"What's The Great Exercise Myth?" you ask. It's perhaps the biggest myth of our time. It's bigger than Zeus. It's bigger than Hercules. Heck, it's even bigger than Big Foot himself. It's the myth of the nineties–the Reebok-Thigh Master-Buns o' Steel Myth. The Myth that says, "Hey, if you want to get into shape, you better be able to wear a size 2 leotard, bounce on the Stairmaster at one hundred miles an hour, and look like Cher." The Myth that never advertises a fitness center by letting you see someone who is even a couple of pounds overweight anywhere near their five thousand dollar tread mills. The Myth that has America convinced that if you want to get in shape, you better already be drop dead gorgeous.

Sorry folks, you've been duped! All of those well tanned, washboard bellied, big haired, Mr. & Ms. Universes you see on TV and at the gym aren't *getting in* shape. They already are there! They're beyond shape. They're cosmetically perfect genetic mutants. God gave them a break. They don't have to get in shape. They just have to stay there. You, however, are out of shape. How would you like to get some back?

Getting in shape is easy. Yes easy! It doesn't require spandex, clapping, or three easy payments of $49.95. All it requires is you. You choose the pace. You choose the exercise. You make the rules. You can do absolutely anything that takes your out of shape body and creates a fat burning, head turning, life yearning machine. ANYTHING! Now that's a lot of options.

Creation–that's the goal of getting in shape. Take one extra pound of flab, exercise it into rock hard muscle, and voila–creation! You just made a more energy efficient, metabolic you: a muscle machine that burns calories. Now you are on your way to creating a better body. What will you do with that extra muscle? Maybe you can use it to hold your head higher, or tuck your tummy in tighter. Either way, people are going to notice, heads are going to turn, and you will start feeling pretty darn good about yourself. But don't stop there. You might as well create a whole new zest for life. Getting in shape means more energy, more concentration, more interests, and more fun! So stop waiting and start creating! Let's take a look at the three basic forms of exercise that will help you create: aerobic, strength training, and stretching.

No Pain, All Gain—Exercise That Doesn't Hurt

Aerobic: According to science, "Active in the presence of oxygen."

Aerobic: According to society, "Gasping for air in the presence of loud music."

Sometime in the last decade, society turned its back on science and decided to invent its own rules for aerobic exercise:

Rule #1   Jump up and down as fast as you can.
Rule #2   Keep jumping until you are completely
           out of breath.
Rule #3   Loud music and lycra burn calories.
Rule #4   No pain. No gain.

What's the net result of these new rules? FAILURE! Complete, utter, miserable, failure. Most compulsive over-eaters are too sore and discouraged from their first aerobic experience to ever try again. Of those few who dare come back for more, nearly half will sustain a significant exercise related injury. Sorry, but sucking wind, breaking bones, and destroying your eardrums are not good ways to get in shape. No pain. No gain. INSANE! So what's the alternative? Well, let's go back to the true definition of **Aerobic**: "Active in the presence of oxygen." It's really that simple. *Action* and *oxygen* are your only two requirements for total aerobic prowess.

Lights, Camera ... ACTION!

If you want to lose weight, you have to move weight. You have to take action. Anytime, anyplace, and anywhere you force your heart to beat faster, your lungs to breathe deeper, and your muscles to move quicker, you're taking action and aerobicising. You don't need state of the art equipment or choreographed dance to get into shape. You just need to move!

For most compulsive overeaters, there's no better way to take action and get in shape than with a nice brisk walk. It's safe, easy to do, requires no special equipment or member-ship fees, and there's very little risk of injury. But best of all, walking works. For example, if you did nothing else to change your lifestyle but briskly walk an extra mile each day, you would burn enough calories to shed 10 pounds a year. Just imagine what walking could do when combined with The Menu For Life—now that's action for you!

O_2 4U

Action and oxygen go hand in hand. You can't exercise aerobically without good old-fashioned oxygen. Don't let Chip, Biff, or Buffy The Fitness Freak tell you any different. The goal of aerobic conditioning is to strengthen your body, not beat it into submission. The moment you hunch over and gasp for air, it's too late. You've lost the benefits of aerobic exercise.

So how can you tell if you're pushing yourself too hard? Try the "talk test." Exercise at a pace that makes you breathe noticeably harder, but still allows you to carry on a conversation. If you exercise alone and don't want to look like a raving lunatic talking to yourself, try softly humming or singing. If it gets too tough to talk, slow down your pace, catch your breath, and then keep moving toward fitness.

Walk Aerobics: Why, How, When, and Where

Why

There are countless reasons to begin a walk aerobics program. The health benefits alone are endless. Exercise helps prevent insomnia, heart disease, high blood pressure, osteoporosis, high cholesterol, constipation, and type II diabetes. Furthermore, the relaxed cadence of a vigorous walk is a great way to increase your stress resistance, improve your concentration, and alleviate any day to day anxiety or depression. But most importantly, every step you take in walk aerobics is a giant leap toward becoming the fat burning machine you long to be. Here's why.

Your metabolic rate is partly a function of muscle mass. Walk aerobics give you muscle; the more muscle you have, the more calories you burn. It's a fact. Better yet, walk aerobics boosts metabolism long after you stop exercising. For example, let's say you walk at the right intensity and for the proper length of time to burn 250 calories. Even though you kick off your Nikes and relax for the night, your metabolism keeps on revving. Over the next eight hours, you will burn and additional 250 calories while you're resting. Not bad, huh? So what are you waiting for? Stop balking and start walking!

How

Start with a good pair of shoes—ones that absorb shock and support your arches. Warm up your heart and muscles with three-to-four minutes of casual walking, then pick up the pace. Walk briskly, breathe deeply, pump your arms, and maintain a nice straight posture. Don't forget the "talk test." Are you too winded to carry on a conversation? Then slow down, but keep walking toward fitness. Never stop abruptly. Always cool down at the end of your workout with another three-to-four minutes of relaxed walking.

If on your first try you can't make it past your driveway without huffing and puffing, that's okay. After all, you can't reverse years of inactivity in a single workout, or even a month's worth. So take it slow, set realistic goals, and try again tomorrow. Gradually increase the intensity and duration of your walks until you can maintain an energetic stride for at least thirty-to-forty minutes. If it takes two months to reach this level, so be it. You'll be healthier two months from now than you are today.

When

A walk a day keeps the doctor away. Make walk aerobics part of your daily routine.

I know what you're thinking. You're thinking, "I don't have time for all this exercise stuff." Well, maybe it's not so much a matter of time, maybe it's just a matter of priorities. You know how it is. Exercise is always the first thing sacrificed whenever conflicts arise—and conflicts always arise.

Admit it, you have hundreds of reasons, explanations, and excuses to sit on your duff; but ninety-nine percent of them are just plain bogus. Stop rationalizing and start exercising! Any exercise is better than none at all. Find cracks in your schedule and fill them with quick workouts. If you can't find a free forty minutes in your day, then split your routine in half and do two twenty-minute workouts. Better yet, do walk aerobics with your family or friends. I can't think of a healthier way to spend quality time with the people you love.

Where

The real beauty of walk aerobics is its versatility. You can do it almost anywhere. Stride around the block, through the neighborhood park, or around the local high school track. If the weather outside is frightful, then the mall is so delightful. Many indoor shopping centers have early morning walking clubs. You can even buy a cheap treadmill and do your walk aerobics at home while watching your favorite TV shows.

Live life aerobically. Be active in the presence of oxygen twenty-four hours a day. Park your car at the end of the lot and walk the rest of the way. Use the stairs instead of the elevator. Take walking breaks instead of coffee breaks. No matter where you are—be it city, town, or suburb; home, work, or on vacation—use the two legs that God gave you and walk yourself fit!

Strength Training: Why, How, When, and Where

Why

Okay, first things first. Toss out that disgusting mental image of some muscle-bound Sluggo with biceps as big as Volkswagens and quit thinking to yourself, "Strength training, no way, I don't want to bulk up!" Of course you don't, and you won't, unless you spend half your waking hours strapped to a bench press. Besides, you've done the bulky thing long enough and hated every minute of it. You don't want to settle for being just a fat burning, head turning, life yearning machine. You want to be a *bulk free*, fat burning, head turning, life yearning machine, and this strength training mumbo jumbo is going to ruin all that, right? Wrong!

Strength training will make you thin! It's a simple matter of physics.

I hated high school physics. I didn't know Isaac Newton from Fig Newton, and it took most of the semester to convince me that a pound of gold weighed the same as a pound of dust bunnies. I mean here's this little bar of gold and this giant box of dust bunnies. How could they possibly weigh the same? I finally got it though—a pound, is a pound, is a pound, no matter how much space it occupies; and so it holds true that a pound of muscle weighs the same as a pound of fat. But here's the kicker—a pound of muscle occupies a lot less space than a pound of fat (about five times less space).

Strength training is like taking a giant box of useless dust bunnies and transforming them into gold. It gives you power, tone, and muscle, while eradicating fat. Create power, and everything in life, from carrying your luggage to shoveling snow, becomes easier. Create tone, and while you're getting in shape, you'll have a shape to get into. Create muscle, and you'll have a more lean, mean, fat burning machine than you ever dreamed possible.

How

Ginghus Khan, Attila the Hun, Napoleon, and all the great warriors throughout history instilled one lone thought into the minds of their conquests, "Resistance is futile!" Futile??? Nonsense! These guys may have been great warriors, but they would make lousy strength trainers. *Resistance*, along with *Form, Extension*, and *Comfort*, are the four principles of successful strength training.

Resistance: Resistance is nothing more than contracting your muscles against force in order to increase power and tone. What force you choose is entirely up to you. It can be weights, elastic bands, water, sand, hills, or even your own body (as with sit-ups and push-ups).

Form: When it comes to strength training, there are only two types of form: good and bad. Bad form is almost everything you see at the gym—backs arching, knees pounding, barbells bouncing, legs jerking, grunting, groaning—all pain and no gain. Good form, on the other hand, is a lot harder to find, but much easier to do. All you need is good posture and proper mechanics. Keep your body straight, and perform all movements in a smooth, controlled fashion. It's that simple.

Extension: Your triceps are made up of hundreds of tiny muscle fibers. Your calves have thousands of them. In fact, each and every muscle in your body is jam-packed with dozens upon dozens of fat burning machines just waiting to ignite. In order to use them all, you have to move them all. A full range of motion is a sure fire way to maximize the strength training of any workout.

Comfort: Whoever replaced "if it feels good, do it" with "no pain, no gain" should be immediately tarred and feathered. Comfort is the key to strength training. As with walk aerobics, your strength training exercises should be demanding, but definitely not painful.

When

Strength train two-to-three times per week. Morning, noon, or night, it really doesn't matter. Just don't strength train two days in a row. Your muscles need a break between sessions to maximize their fat burning efficiency.

Where

Wherever you want. Strength training may be even more versatile than walk aerobics. You can join a gym, buy a home fitness system, or purchase a couple of inexpensive dumbbells and follow the exercises listed at the end of this chapter. For a refreshing change of pace, try swimming. Water is liquid resistance—a great way to balance strength training with an aerobic workout. Better yet, why not combine strength training with your walk aerobics program. You can strengthen your legs by adding the resistance of a good steep hill to your walk; or give your upper body the

workout of a lifetime by pumping your arms while holding
a pair of light barbells (1-3 pounds). Yes indeed, no matter
where you are or where you're going, strength training will
get you there, inch by fat burning inch–guaranteed!

Stretching: Why, How, When, and Where

Why

How do you kick off your day? With a nice long shower,
a piping hot cup of java, or a glance at the morning news?
Nah, maybe that's how you think your day begins, but I'll
bet you're forgetting the real key to clearing those morning
cobwebs–a nice long stretch. Don't deny it. No matter how
avant-garde you are, you love that dawn's early light stretch
just like everyone else. Why? Is it because stretching makes
you taller and thinner? Not a chance. Maybe it's because
stretching gives you Herculean strength and a model like
figure? Nope, wrong again. "Then why bother?" you ask.
Well, it's simple. Stretching feels good, and that's all the
reason you need.

Forget the fact that flexibility training prevents the
aches, pains, pulls, and strains of the active life you'll be
leading. Stretching just feels good. It's a brief moment in
time when you give full attention to your mind and body,
and release the stress in those new found muscles of yours.
It's your time to feel wonderfully relaxed. Now that's a feeling you definitely deserve.

How

Don't settle for just touching your toes. Let flexibility be
a total body experience. Start each stretch with a long cleansing breath, then slowly exhale as you complete the movement. Remember to apply form, extension, and comfort.
They are just as important here as they were in strength
training.

Stretch gradually to the point of tension, never to the
point of pain. Hold your stretch for at least ten seconds and

don't bounce, DON'T BOUNCE, for goodness sakes, **DON'T BOUNCE!**

Most of all, relax and have fun. Why not try yoga or tai chi. You'll be glad you did. But if you're pressed for time, and quite frankly who isn't, just turn to the Appendix and try the Ten Minute Flexercise.

When

Anytime will do. If you can't fit ten straight minutes of flexercise into your schedule, then squeeze it in whenever you can. Take short "stretch breaks" throughout the day. That's a surefire stress buster and a great way to refocus your energy.

Of course if you're really looking to get limber–I mean the kind of flexibility that would make Gumby jealous–try stretching at the end of your walk aerobics.

"Stretch at the end of my walk aerobics," you say, "Don't you mean at the beginning?"

I know, this goes against everything you learned in gym class, but Jocko the Gym Teacher was wrong. Things stretch farther when they are warm. You know that, even if Jocko doesn't. Rubber, elastic, muscle–it's all the same. If it's going to stretch, it's going to stretch farther, easier, and safer when it's warm. Muscle, in particular, stretches an extra five percent when it's warm. So save the pre-workout stretching for Jocko. Warm up by walking slowly, then pick up the pace. Wait until your muscles are warm, then, go ahead and S T R E T C H !

Where

Anywhere that's toasty, comfortable, and quiet. Cold tile floors and noisy backgrounds just won't do. Think warm, think heat, think Florida. Flexercise someplace that is warm enough to keep your muscles loose and your stretch maximized.

Don't forget to treat your body right. Stretch using an exercise mat, several plushy towels, or at least make sure there's plenty of nice soft carpeting to cushion your body.

Last, but definitely not least, pick a place that offers sanctuary from the hustle and bustle of everyday life—a nice tranquil spot that lets you unwind and reflect on the most important person in the world—YOU!

The Menu For Strength

Here are just a few of the many strength training exercises that will firm, tone, and shape you, but definitely won't bulk you up. When using weights, remember to start light and add weight gradually over time. (Consult your physician before starting any exercise program.)

Crunches

<u>Resistance</u>: Upper and Lower Abdominal Muscles

<u>Form</u>: Lie on your back with your knees bent and feet spread approximately one foot apart. Lightly intertwine your hands and place them behind your head to relax the neck. Keep your elbows pointed to the sides, not forward, and maintain a straight lined posture (don't rest your chin on your chest).

<u>Extension</u>: Using your abdominal muscles, gradually raise your torso 30-45 degrees off the floor and slowly return to the starting position.

<u>Comfort</u>: Repeat until maintaining proper form or extension becomes difficult. (Never pull on your neck. Your hands should be used only for support.)

Reverse Crunches

<u>Resistance</u>: Upper and Lower Abdominal Muscles

<u>Form</u>: Lie on your back with your legs bent and knees together. Place your arms down at the sides of your thighs with your palms resting on the floor.

<u>Extension</u>: Gradually bring your knees in toward your chest, lifting your hips approximately four inches off the ground and then slowly return your feet to the floor.

<u>Comfort</u>: Repeat until maintaining proper form or extension becomes difficult.

Dumbbell Press

<u>Resistance</u>: Pectoral Muscles

<u>Form</u>: Lie on the floor with your knees bent. Bend your arms like chicken wings, and hold the weights by your sides at chest level.

<u>Extension</u>: Slowly lift the weights off the floor, extending your arms straight above your body. Avoid locking your elbows. Gradually lower the weights back down to your chest until your elbows touch the floor.

<u>Comfort</u>: Adjust weight until you can perform 12-16 repetitions with proper form and extension.

Seated Dumbbell Row

<u>Resistance</u>: Deltoids, Trapezius, and Latissimus Dorsi

<u>Form</u>: Sit in a chair with your feet spaced comfortably apart. Lean forward from the waist, and keep your back straight and head looking forward. Place one weight in each hand and extend both of your arms toward the floor with your palms facing backward.

<u>Extension</u>: Bend your elbows, and slowly lift the weight as if you were trying to touch the backs of your shoulders together. Gradually lower the weights to the starting position.

<u>Comfort</u>: Adjust weight until you can perform 12-16 repetitions with proper form and extension.

Dumbbell Shrugs

<u>Resistance</u>: Trapezius and Deltoids

<u>Form</u>: Stand straight with your feet spaced comfortably apart. Hold the dumbbells straight down at your sides.

<u>Extension</u>: Raise your shoulders up and rotate them in a circular motion from front to back for a full set. Repeat motion in the reverse direction.

Comfort: Adjust weight until you can perform 12-16 repetitions with proper form and extension.

Biceps Dumbbell Curl

Resistance: Biceps

Form: Stand straight with your feet spaced comfortably apart. Hold the dumbbells at your sides with your palms facing forward and your arms fully extended. Keep elbows close to your waist at all times.

Extension: Slowly curl both dumbbells up to the chest at the same time. Next, gradually lower dumbbells back to the starting position and repeat.

Comfort: Adjust weight until you can perform 12-16 repetitions with proper form and extension.

Triceps Dumbbell Extension

Resistance: Triceps

Form: Stand straight with your feet spaced comfortably apart. Hold a single dumbbell with both hands interlocked around the end of the weight. Raise the weight above your head with your palms facing upward. Avoid locking elbows.

Extension: Bend your elbows and slowly lower weight behind your head toward the center of your back, keeping your elbows close to your head and pointed upward. Gradually lift dumbbell back to the starting position.

Comfort: Adjust weight until you can perform 12-16 repetitions with proper form and extension.

Butt Toner

Resistance: Gluteus Maximus (use ankle weights)

Form: Stand facing a wall. For balance, rest your hands against the wall at chest level. Maintain a straight relaxed posture with your feet spaced comfortably apart.

Extension: Slowly extend your right leg backward as if trying to touch your toes to the other side of the room. Gradually return to the starting position. Complete an entire set and repeat with the opposite leg.

Comfort: Adjust weight until you can perform 12-16 repetitions with proper form and extension.

Seated Leg Extension

Resistance: Quadriceps (use ankle weights)

Form: Sit in a chair with your feet flat on the floor and your back straight. Balance yourself by grasping the sides of the chair.

Extension: Slowly extend your right leg until your knee almost, but doesn't quite, lock. Gradually return to the starting position. Complete an entire set and repeat with the opposite leg.

Comfort: Adjust weight until you can perform 12-16 repetitions with proper form and extension.

Hamstring Curl

Resistance: Hamstrings (use ankle weights)

Form: Stand facing a wall. For balance, rest your hands against the wall at chest level. Maintain a straight relaxed posture with your feet spaced comfortably apart.

Extension: Slowly bend your right leg, lifting your heel to your buttocks. Gradually return to the starting position. Complete an entire set and repeat with the opposite leg.

Comfort: Adjust weight until you can perform 12-16 repetitions with proper form and extension.

The Ten Minute Flexercise

Standing Neck Stretches

1. Stretch your neck from side to side. Try touching your ears to your shoulders. Hold for at least ten seconds.
2. Try to touch your chin to your chest without opening your mouth. Hold for at least ten seconds.
3. Twist your head from side to side in a slow, exaggerated "NO" motion.

Standing Tree Stretch

Interlace your fingers in front of your waist. Turn palms outward. Raise your arms overhead and slowly straighten your elbows. Hold for at least ten seconds.

Standing Chest Stretch

Interlace fingers behind your waist. Turn palms outward. Slowly extend hands out and away from your body, trying to press your shoulder blades together. Hold for ten seconds.

Standing Shoulder Stretch

Reach one hand behind your head and give yourself a pat on the back. To extend the stretch, take your other hand and gently press back on your tricep. Hold for at least ten seconds. Repeat with opposite shoulder.

Standing Side Benders

Place your hands on your hips. Lean to the left. Stretch your left elbow toward the floor. Hold for at least ten seconds, then repeat to the right.

Standing Side Twisters

Place your hands on your hips. Hold your hips still and rotate your entire upper body to the left. Hold for at least ten seconds. Repeat to the right.

Cannon Ball Stretch

Lie on your back. Take both knees and slowly pull them toward your chest. Hold for at least ten seconds.

Quadriceps Stretch

Lie on your stomach and grasp your right foot with your right hand. Slowly pull your heel to your buttocks. Hold for at least ten seconds. Repeat with your left leg.

Hamstring Stretch

Sit on the floor. Bring your right foot in toward your groin. Keep your left leg straight and slowly lean forward, attempting to touch your left foot. Hold for at least ten seconds. Repeat to the right.

Butterfly Stretch

Sit on the floor. Bend your legs and pull the soles of your feet in toward your groin. Grasp your feet and lean forward, pressing your forearms on your shins. Hold for at least ten seconds.

Standing Calf Stretch

Keep your feet flat on the ground. Place your hands on a wall and lean in, slowly stretching your calves. Hold for at least ten seconds.

Appendix

Desirable Weight In Pounds, Adults 25+

FRAME

WOMEN	Small	Medium	Large
4-10	86	95	104
4-11	88	98	107
5-0	90	100	110
5-1	95	105	115
5-2	99	110	121
5-3	104	115	126
5-4	108	120	132
5-5	113	125	137
5-6	117	130	143
5-7	122	135	148
5-8	127	140	154
5-9	131	145	159
5-10	135	150	165
5-11	140	155	170
6-0	144	160	176

Desirable Weight In Pounds, Adults 25+

FRAME

MEN	Small	Medium	Large
5-2	106	118	130
5-3	112	124	136
5-4	117	130	143
5-5	123	136	149
5-6	128	142	156
5-7	134	148	162
5-8	139	154	169
5-9	144	160	176
5-10	150	166	182
5-11	155	172	189
6-0	161	178	196
6-1	166	184	202
6-2	171	190	209
6-3	177	196	215
6-4	182	202	222

Index

Order Form

Send: CHOCOLATE...
IS MY KRYPTONITE
To family and friends

To: _____

Address: _____

City: _____State: _____Zip: _____

From: _____

Address: _____

City: _____State: _____Zip: _____

Payment:
Send $12.95 via check or money order to:

Saguaro Publishing
P.O. Box 457
Litchfield Park, AZ 85340

Credit card orders call toll-free 1-888-561-3095. Have
your Visa, MasterCard, or Diners Club card ready.

Sales tax:
Please add 5.75% for books shipped to Arizona addresses.

Shipping/Handling:
Add $3.50 for the first book and $2.00 for each additional
book. Please allow 4-6 weeks for delivery.

Order Form

Send: **CHOCOLATE...**
IS MY KRYPTONITE

To family and friends

To: _____

Address: _____

City: _____State: _____Zip: _____

From: _____

Address: _____

City: _____State: _____Zip: _____

Payment:
Send $12.95 via check or money order to:

Saguaro Publishing
P.O. Box 457
Litchfield Park, AZ 85340

Credit card orders call toll-free 1-888-561-3095. Have
your Visa, MasterCard, or Diners Club card ready.

Sales tax:
Please add 5.75% for books shipped to Arizona addresses.

Shipping/Handling:
Add $3.50 for the first book and $2.00 for each additional
book. Please allow 4-6 weeks for delivery.